First-Time Coach
Youth Football

Scott Tappa

Iola-Scandinavia Pee Wee Athletics

© 2019 Scott Tappa. All rights reserved.

No part of this book may be reproduced, stored in a retrieval system or transmitted, in any form or by any means, electronic, mechanical, photocopying, recording, or otherwise, without prior permission of Scott Tappa

Cover photos: Jana Tappa

Interior photos: Jana Tappa, Danielle Taggart, Steven Soik

scott_tappa@hotmail.com

twitter.com/scotttappa

facebook.com/isfirebirds

To Dad, who showed me why kids need coaches

To Mom, who inspired a love of books and reading

To Jana, who created the perfect environment for coaches

To Will and Charlie, who made me a coach

To all of the kids I've coached and guys I've coached with — once a Firebird, always a Firebird

TABLE OF CONTENTS

Dedication 5

Preface 9

Introduction 10

Preseason 18

Practice Planning 35

Offense 60

Defense /Special Teams 88

Game Day 104

Postseason /Offseason 122

Forward Pass 128

Resources 130

12 Simple Plays 134

PREFACE

It was a forgettable July evening in 1980-something, and I was an 11-year-old playing in a forgettable Little League game. My team was slogging through a forgettable summer of baseball, and I was sitting on the bench as the opposing pitcher struggled to find the strike zone. The lethargy was broken by two of my more knuckleheaded teammates.

A kid on the other team had a brother who had an intellectual disability, and my teammates were teasing him from their seats on the bench. My dad, our head coach, heard their cackling and charged into the dugout from coaching the bases and gave my teammates a tongue lashing. The teasing stopped. After the game he talked with us about why what our teammates had done was wrong.

Should have been obvious, right? But 11-year-olds accustomed to casually hearing derogatory terms for the intellectually disabled thrown around at the ballfield, playground, and other places may not have ever considered such words or actions to be wrong. Dad made clear that it was. It was a lesson in empathy.

Like a lot of kids, I was obsessed with sports growing up. Played all of them, watched all of them, read about all of them. Of the hundreds of days and thousands of hours I spent at practices and games, the events of that July evening stuck with me more than anything else a coach said. Is that influenced by the fact it was my dad? Of course. But more importantly, it was because he was my coach.

That's why, as you read this book, remember that years from now the children you coach won't remember much, if anything, about the X's and O's, techniques, or other parts of their youth sports experience. But if you do it right, they'll remember that you were a good person and helped them become a good one too.

PART 1

Introduction

Sure, I'll do it.

Gulp.

Congratulations! You've just agreed to coach a youth football team! Waiting for you are 20 children looking forward to playing the greatest team sport ever invented. Your task is to teach them the fundamentals of the game, foster an appreciation for hard work and commitment, and make sure they are having fun — and most importantly, keep them safe. To these 8-year-olds, you are Bill Belichick, John Madden, Vince Lombardi.

But you've never coached football, and the last time you played tackle football was ninth grade.

Gulp.

Fear not! Thousands of men and women have gone before you in this journey and lived to tell about it. Some thrived, finding coaching to be one of the most rewarding experiences of their lives. Some merely survived, limping through several months of misery and returning to the bleachers. This guide will help you fall into the first category.

If you are a seasoned youth football coach looking for another perspective on how it's done, welcome! We applaud your continued search for knowledge. But this book really isn't meant for you. It is meant for adults:

- Who enjoy football and may have helped out with intramural grade school sports — soccer, tee ball, flag football, etc. — and whose organized football playing experience ended in high school if not earlier. Youth tackle football is a far more complex endeavor.

- Who have served as an assistant football coach at a higher level like college or high school, but are unfamiliar with the idiosyncrasies of coaching little kids. No need for talk of 3 techniques or pattern match coverage. Your players are more interested in whether or not they will be running relays at the end of practice.

Sound like you? Great, let's proceed.

What This Book Is About

Before diving in, let's take a few paragraphs to summarize what we hope to cover in these pages.

Preseason planning. If you think you can show up on the first day of practice with a few random thoughts scribbled on a piece of paper, think again. A few hours of summer planning and communication can go a long way toward ensuring your season gets off to a good start and stays positive throughout.

Practice planning. For many coaches and children, tackle football is their first athletic experience involving extensive practice time. Rightfully so, as football is a rich, complicated sport with a seemingly endless amount of things to learn. Poor or non-existent planning can lead to long, boring, unproductive practices. Detailed planning yields high-energy practices that balance skill development with team work, with so much accomplished that the hours fly by.

Offense. If you have ever played Madden (or for readers of a certain age, Tecmo Bowl), you have been an offensive coordinator. But when those X's and O's are someone's son or daughter it is an entirely different story. We share offensive concepts appropriate for 8- through 12-year-olds.

Defense. Not as complicated as offense, right? Even if the opposing quarterback isn't Aaron Rodgers, one or two missed assignments can often result in big plays going the other way. Learn some straightforward tips on assembling a sound youth football defense.

Game day preparation. Anyone who ends up coaching youth football has probably watched hundreds of football games. If you're honest, you have probably questioned coaching decisions once or twice! You will regret those times when you besmirched your team's coaching choices the first time you try to make a third down play call while a 60-pound third grader tugs on your arm and asks if he can play safety. Put systems in place to ensure the chaos of gameday is as manageable as possible.

End of season/offseason. When the final whistle blows don't just throw your clipboard in the closet and forget about it until next summer. Reflect on the completed season and stay engaged with your kids and families.

What This Book Is Not About

While we're at it, let's make clear what this book will not cover in great detail.

General coaching and teaching philosophy. Over the years I have coached football, basketball, baseball, and other sports, and in preparation have read as much as possible about doing it well. Millions of words have been written about how to best teach and coach young people. While bits and pieces of accumulated coaching philosophy will appear throughout these pages, there is no way we could do justice the body of work available covering this subject.

Program development. While I have served as president of my local organization for several years, as well as the president of the conference to which we belong, program-level topics will receive only brief mention in these pages. To be clear, marketing and promotion, fund raising, community relationships, and other activities are vitally important. Without them you would not have a team to coach. But this book will focus on what I consider to be the fun stuff!

Advanced football strategy. As a long-time subscriber to the website X&O Labs, connoisseur of Coaches Choice videos, reader of Chris Brown's Smart Football, and general carnivore for all things football strategy, it is with reluctance that I will admit that this is not a deep dive into football tactics. Football nerds are certainly welcome to join us, with the understanding that a great deal of their technical know-how will not be appropriate for players of a certain age.

Comprehensive playbooks. We will give you a few simple ideas for setting up an offense and defense. You can take it from there, either adapting and building upon these concepts or choosing something else entirely. If you are interested in diving deeper into X's and O's, consider obtaining a copy of my companion book, *114 Youth Football Plays*.

Drill catalogs. There are hundreds of valid drills for developing football skills. While we may reference a few, as with playbooks we encourage you to explore other sources online or in print to find ones that fit your players and coaching staff. If you need somewhere to start, consider visiting my YouTube channel, which among other youth football content has a variety of practice drills for blocking, tackling, and position groups.

Know the Rules

Most casual football fans would know the rule differences between college and the NFL: two-minute warning, clock stoppages after first downs, overtime guidelines, etc. By comparison, the rules for most youth football leagues are dramatically different than what you are used to seeing on Saturday and Sunday. Before starting practice, familiarize yourself with the details of the league in which your team competes.

The program for which I coach, Iola-Scandinavia Pee Wee Athletics, competes in the Mid-State Youth Football and Cheerleading Conference. Here are some of the rules Mid-State teams play by.

- A player's weight determines whether or not they are "restricted" and as such limited to certain positions on the offensive and defensive line. At the Mid-State Junior Pee Wee level (primarily third and fourth graders), players 108 pounds or heavier may only play defensive tackle, offensive tackle, or center. At the Pee Wee level (primarily fifth and sixth graders), the restricted weight is 138 pounds.

- Every player must play at least seven plays per half, not including point-after touchdown kicks.

- Linebackers and cornerbacks may not line up closer than 3 yards to the line of scrimmage, except when the opposing team possesses the ball inside the defensive team's 10-yard-line. No more than three linebackers are allowed to line up inside the box — the area between

the offensive tackles' outside shoulders. No pre-snap blitzing is allowed.

- Defensive tackles and nose tackles may only align head up on the offensive linemen across from them.

- Junior Pee Wee games do not include kickoffs; at the start of halves and after scores teams assume possession at their own 40-yard-line. Punts are allowed, but the play is dead when the ball is contacted by the receiving team.

- Quarters are eight minutes long.

- Successful point-after touchdown kicks are worth two points. Other successful PAT attempts are worth one point.

- Teams are limited to 10 hours of practice per week before Labor Day and six hours of practice per week after Labor Day.

These rules (which along with other Mid-State guidelines help inform many of the perspectives shared on the pages ahead) are meant to ensure a fair, safe playing environment for conference football teams and have been developed over the course of nearly 20 years. Commit to learning your league's rules inside and out — they will have a significant effect on your team's strategy and personnel deployment.

Know Yourself

No two youth football conferences are exactly alike, nor are any two communities' organizations. Teams and leagues take on all sorts of shapes and sizes: Urban. Small town. Select. Everyone plays. Eight-year-olds. Middle schoolers. Tackle. Flag. Rookie Tackle. What are you?

For instance, here are details about the organization and conference in which I have coached for many years.

- Mid-State consists of 14 Central Wisconsin communities that could be considered rural or small town. The conference has been in existence for nearly 20 years. The high schools our programs feed range in size from roughly 100 to 500 students. Many of our communities' high school programs are among the best in Wisconsin among smaller schools.

- Teams compete at two age levels: Junior Pee Wee, which is primarily 8- and 9-year-olds or third and fourth graders; and Pee Wee, which is primarily 10- and 11-year-olds or fifth and sixth graders. A limited number of lighter 10-year-olds are eligible to play on Junior Pee Wee teams.

- The majority of Mid-State communities field one team at each age level, although larger ones regularly field multiple teams. Teams do not play other teams from their own community.

- For the past few years our Iola-Scandinavia program has included 45-50 football players evenly divided between the two age levels. Prior to that, we typically fielded three teams, two at one level and one at the other. Dividing our kids up evenly among multiple teams at an age level was a tremendously difficult task and always fraught with internal controversy and stress. We are a no-cut organization, everyone who registers is given the opportunity to play.

- Junior Pee Wee teams play six regular season games with no playoffs. Pee Wee teams play six regular season games, with the potential to play one or two playoff games. Our season runs from August to October. Games are played Saturdays at our communities' high school fields.

That is what I know, and the framework for the observations, experiences, and insights shared in the pages ahead. Chances are your situation is not 100 percent the same. Even so, we think you will find a lot of good nuggets here to use with your program.

Let's go!

PART 2

Preseason

On July 4, most people are enjoying fireworks, parades, and get-togethers with friends and families. Youth football coaches are grilling burgers and other succulent meats, enjoying a few adult beverages, and considering the following.

- What offense and defense will we be running this season?

- What are we going to do the first couple weeks in practice?

- Do we have the right equipment?

- How does the practice field look?

- Who is helping me coach this year?

- Do my players and their families know what to expect this season?

- Who has the ketchup?

It is the Fourth of July, after all! You still have almost a month left until your season starts, and if you have not yet considered the above questions, don't worry — there is still time. But do not wait too much longer to start planning. Heading into a season unprepared is a certain recipe for an unproductive August and unsatisfying September.

In this chapter, we will not cover offense, defense, or practice planning. Those topics are sufficiently important and detailed to merit their own chapter later. We will, however, examine communication with families, setting up your coaching staff, and equipment and other practice conditions. And if there are enough pages left over, we will rank our favorite summer beers.

Communication

If you take nothing else away from this chapter, let it be this: a youth sports coach can never communicate too much with players and their families. As someone who ended up coaching, you are probably the type of person who takes it upon themselves to stay in the loop on your kids' practice and game times, equipment requirements, and other happenings. But not everyone is like you! While your football team is the center of your world (at least for a few months), it may rank pretty far down the totem pole for a parent juggling their child's school, church, family, and other sports obligations. Rather than lament and complain about this fact, take it upon yourself to do everything in your power to arm parents with all of the pertinent information they and their child

Last Game

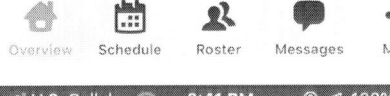

From: Coach Rice

Make sure everyone is watering up right now. Plus if you have an extra water bottle bring it. Should start cooling down a little by the time the game starts.
See you in 3 hours and GO BIRDS!

Two examples of TeamSnap communication

need.

When my older son started tackle football, the communication we received from this organization and his coach was primarily paper-based and word of mouth. His team assignment and information regarding the start of practice arrived in the mail. In-season updates were small strips of paper handed to players after practice. We have come a long way since then! Here are four tools for communicating with a large group.

Email: Pros — Established communication medium. Good for longer messages containing lots of information. Best for sharing attachments. Cons — Every season there will be at least a handful of parents who do not have an email address, and a few more who have email but do not regularly check it.

Facebook: Pros — Most people have Facebook accounts (may be a con?!). Group messaging or private groups are accessible by phone, tablet, or computer. Group communication can be complemented by a public-facing Facebook page featuring photos, video, events, and other

Scott Tappa   21

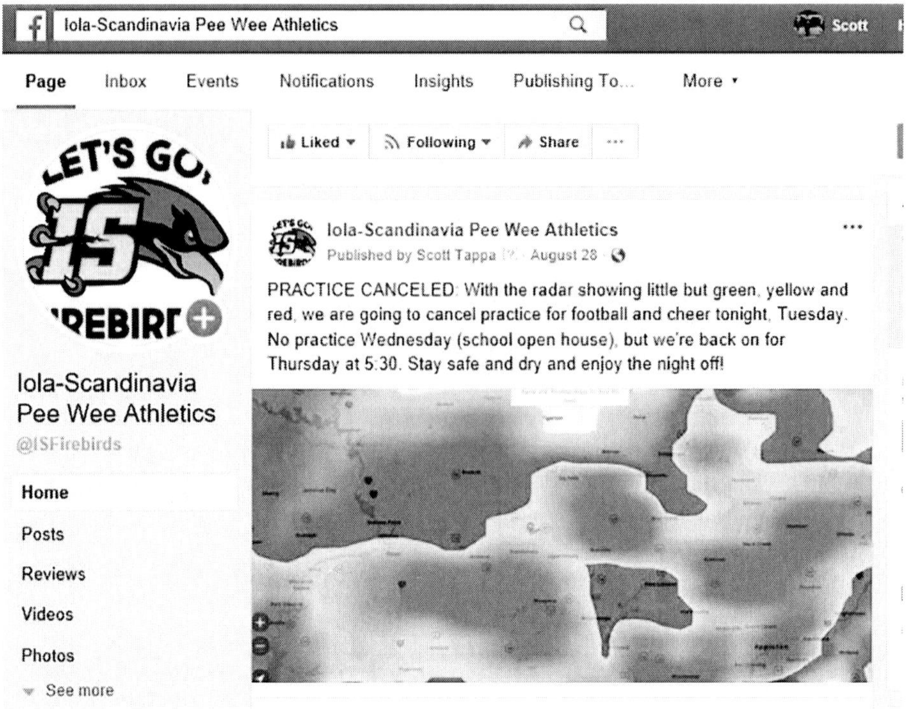

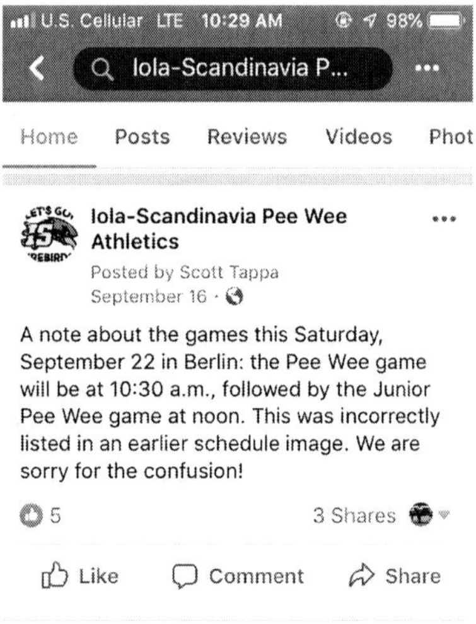

Three examples of Facebook communication

First-Time Coach: Youth Football

announcements. Cons — Many people consider Facebook a necessary evil and prefer to spend as little time there as possible.

Text: Pros — Everyone has mobile phones. Everyone has their phone on them at all times. Everyone texts. Cons — Some people may not be able to properly take part in group texts because of their carriers' settings. Can be difficult to send attachments.

TeamSnap: Pros — Designed specifically for teams to communicate. Wide range of sports-specific features. Accessible from phone, tablet, or computer. Cons — Multiple communication options within app can be difficult to keep straight. Free option has limited functionality, additional features come at a cost.

These are certainly not the only means of communication that exist, and with time you will learn what communication methods work best for your team. You will likely find that 90 percent of your families are fine using your preferred method, but a handful will communicate with you in another way. This can be frustrating, but acknowledging families' communication preferences or capabilities can go a long way toward ensuring a healthy dialogue.

When to Start

The minute that Fourth of July barbecue is done! Kidding of course, but let's think about the appropriate time to start formally communicating with your entire team. We will assume that your team begins practice August 1 after holding registration no later than April or early May.

If your organization has multiple football teams (or in the case of my organization also a cheer team), critical information regarding the upcoming season should begin with the organization's leadership sometime in late spring/early summer. Key items that apply to all children participating include making sure necessary paperwork has been filed, volunteer or fundraising opportunities, equipment handout, practice start date, picture day date, first game date, and more. This information should be communicated as soon as possible, as many families plan vacations around the time you will be starting practice. They need to know the ramifications of their child missing time early in the season.

Your organization's leadership should provide you with a roster, complete with as much family contact information as possible, no later than the first week in July. Team-specific information should be communicated shortly thereafter (right after you finish cleaning the grill). Consider using email for this initial message, in which you can steer families to your preferred method of team-wide communication, and collect other email addresses and phone numbers for parents who want to stay in the loop.

What else to include in this first message? Not too much. Introduce yourself and your coaches. Let them know how to best contact you. Reiterate the date, time, and location of equipment handout, where you can deliver more information in a face-to-face setting. Specify the date, time, and location of the first couple weeks of practices. Lay out any equipment, like shoes or mouthguards, that families may need to purchase before the start of practice. That should be sufficient — be thorough without being overwhelming.

Your next formal contact with families should be at equipment handout. We will address this event in more detail later, but specific to family communication, use this time to meet your players and their parents face-to-face. Some of these people may be old friends or acquaintances. Others may be complete strangers to you. Equipment handout is an opportunity to start bringing both groups together to build a new family — your team. As in the introductory email, introduce yourself and your coaches and go over key dates. Be clear about the best way to contact you. Talk about your philosophy and hopes for the season. Lay out your discipline policy — be thorough and specific, and do not make rules up as the season goes along.

You might also use this opportunity to start teaching football to your kids.

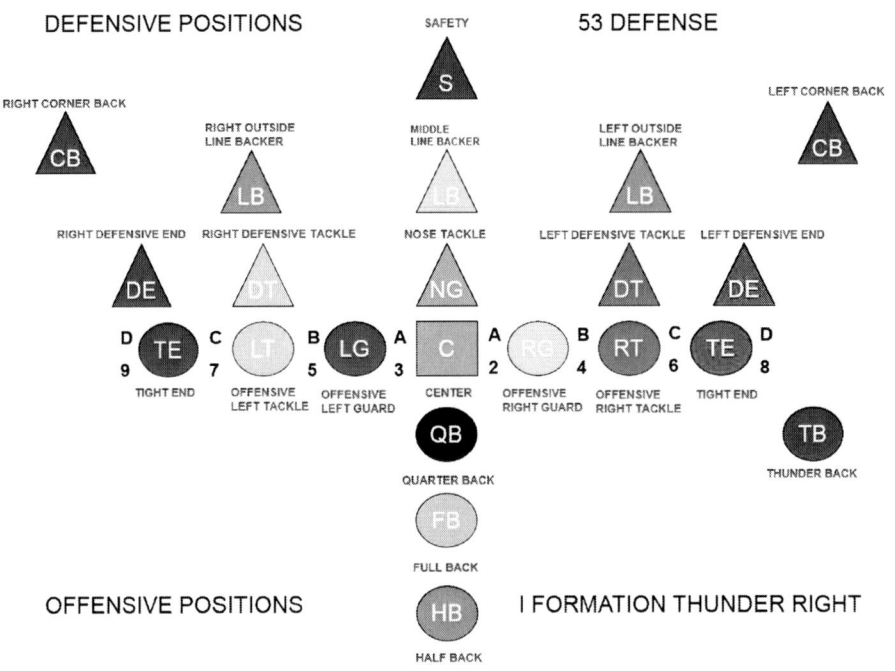

Examples of handouts for registration or equipment distribution

OFFENSIVE HOLE NUMBERING

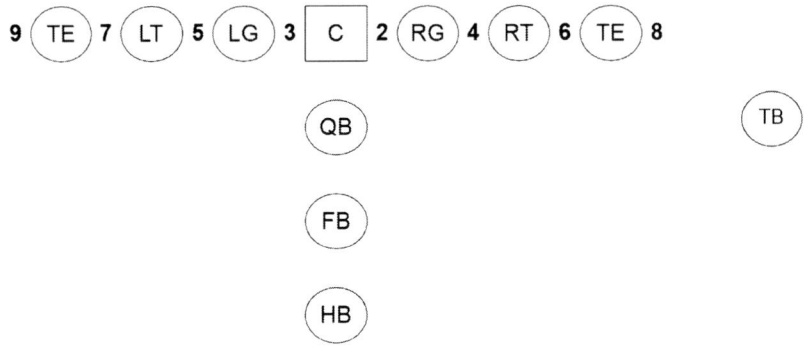

New players could benefit from a one-page handout illustrating basics like hole numbers or gap letters, positions, etc. This could ease some of their anxiety about playing and help them get off to a better start. Returning players could benefit from a look at new play diagrams. They might be ready to move on from baseball and get excited about the new wrinkles you will be using. Use your best judgment about what is appropriate for these kids at this time.

Once the season starts, team-wide messages should not be necessary more than once per week. A message Sunday or Monday reviewing that week's practice days and times, the location and time of the weekend's game, and any other pertinent news or reminders will help keep everyone on the same page. Consistent and thorough communication on the front end goes a long way toward mitigating potential problems.

Working With Parents

It is hard to read anything about youth sports these days without coming across a reference to problematic parents. Without rehashing or summarizing all of the horror stories making their way around the Internet, I am here to reassure you: it does not need to be a "problem!" Maybe we have been unusually blessed or lucky, but in my time coaching youth sports our teams have had a minimum of issues with parents causing problems.

That is not to say it has been smooth sailing 100 percent of the time. Far from it! Any time you take 25 children of varying maturity and skill levels, place them in an environment as physically and emotionally charged as tackle football, and spend 5-10 hours a week together, there are bound to be bumps in the road. But by taking a few simple steps you can keep these issues to a minimum.

Communicate, communicate, communicate! This can't be stressed enough. The more you communicate with your players' families, the more you can demonstrate that you care about their kids and are putting thought and energy into ensuring their football experience is positive. Establishing lines

of communication and keeping them open ensures they have an outlet for bringing concerns to you as they arise, rather than letting them fester internally or manifesting themselves as gossip.

Involve them. The most common way to do this is by making parents part of your coaching staff (more on that in a bit). But there are lots of other ways to involve parents. A "team parent" can coordinate activities like handing out apparel or picture orders, post-practice birthday treats, or other non-football functions. Videographers or photographers can add immense value to your operation. A health and safety coordinator can be sure your medical kit is up to date, advise on safety concerns, and generally reassure other parents that safety is a top priority for your team. Be creative, and don't be shy about asking. Lots of people want to help, but don't know where help is needed and are shy about asking.

Don't be a jerk. Obvious, right? Unfortunately, youth sports are littered with coaches who demean their kids verbally, punish them unfairly, or worse. Be better than that. This is not to suggest that kids can not be coached "hard." If criticism is fair, well-reasoned, not personal, and properly explained, getting on a kid can be beneficial for him. The problem lies with hard coaching that singles players out unfairly, is not consistent with coaching of other players, uses vulgar language, or is the result of coaching, teaching, or communication mistakes that are your responsibility. This applies to how you treat your fellow coaches, parents, officials, opposing players and coaches, the chain gang, concession stand workers ... you get the point. Don't be a jerk.

Follow these steps and you won't be "dealing" with parents, you will be "working" with parents.

Assembling Your Staff

You are coaching youth football for the first time. You need help. Even if you were the reincarnation of Bear Bryant, you would need help. There are too many players, too many positions, too many individual skills involved in football for someone to coach by themselves. You need a coaching staff.

Who will help you? Most likely, a handful of your players' fathers. Maybe uncles, mothers, grandparents, or brothers, but the overwhelming source of volunteer help for your team will be your families. If you can enlist a veteran coach or local college or high school student to assist you, that is fantastic (and my guess is more common in larger-population communities than the one in which I live and coach).

Most likely, the brave souls who step forward to help you will vary greatly in their coaching experience, football knowledge, and commitment to learning both. Some may show up 30 minutes before practice, others may miss half the games because they work some weekends. Some may be gregarious go-getters, others may be introverts who prefer to work in the background. Thinking creatively and comprehensively, you can find a role for all of these people to add value to your team.

Start by getting to know more about your coaches. Chances are you know some of them already but have not spoken extensively about coaching football. Learn more about their experiences and motivation for coaching. Maybe one guy played running back in high school and feels comfortable coaching that position. Maybe another guy never played a snap of organized ball but has a big boy, and wants to help coach him on the offensive line. Everyone has a different story — figure out how they fit together to help you out. Here is a one example of how six coaches could be deployed for a team of 20-25 kids.

- The head coach coordinates one side of the ball. For the sake of this example, let's say he serves as offensive coordinator, designing the offense, installing and teaching plays, calling plays on game day.

- In addition to coordinating, the head coach also coaches a position group. The natural inclination is to assume he takes the quarterbacks and running backs, and that would not be a bad choice. But do not underestimate the importance of offensive line play — a head coach's time would be well spent ensuring that group gets maximum attention.

- With this hypothetical team and coaching staff, allot two coaches to backs and receivers and three coaches to the offensive line. The coach assigned defensive coordinator duties serves as a floater, filling in wherever he is needed.

- While a head coach can certainly coordinate both offense and defense, each carries substantial enough practice planning and game day responsibilities to merit its own coordinator. In our scenario, with the head coach overseeing the offense, a different coach serves as defensive coordinator.

- Similar to offensive position coaching, it is logical that the defensive coordinator would coach the linebackers; we often refer to the middle linebacker as the quarterback of the defense. But consider devoting the head coach's attention to defensive ends, who are arguably the most important players on your defense (more on this later).

- With this hypothetical team and coaching staff, allot two coaches to defensive tackles and nose tackles, one coach to defensive ends, and three coaches to linebackers and defensive backs.

- For special teams, put a separate coach not coordinating either offense or defense in charge of organizing kickoff and kickoff return teams. Defensive coordinator oversees punt return, and offensive coordinator oversees the punt team (if you punt ... which you shouldn't ... more on that later!).

- Other specific, critical tasks that can be assigned to assistant coaches include leading warmups and individual skill-building circuits like tackling and blocking, counting plays during games, or even serving as practice DJ.

Many times these roles will change and evolve over time, as you and your staff learn more about each other, your strengths and weaknesses, your availability, and your team's needs. Plan, but be flexible.

Before the season starts, be sure to communicate with each of your coaches what role you would like them to fill, and be sure they are comfortable with it. Share as much of the broad strategic philosophies you plan to implement. If there are certain ways you would like individual skills to be taught — tackling, blocking, snapping — be sure to discuss this with position coaches. Suggest

techniques to cover and sources for practice drills pertaining to every position.

Coach your coaches.

Equipment

Practicing and playing tackle football requires more equipment than any other youth sport, save perhaps expensive sports like ice hockey and lacrosse. While you will not need every single item listed here from Day 1, or at every practice, or some ever, the more you can provide, the better.

Individual equipment: Our organization provides players with helmets, shoulder pads, pants, practice jerseys, and mouth guards. We size kids for each of these items at spring registration and assemble equipment bags a week or so before practice starts. Holding an equipment distribution night before the start of practice, in addition to being a great way to meet your kids and families, can also save a lot of time the first couple nights of practice — kids grow, shrink, cut their hair, grow their hair, or were just plain incorrectly measured at registration.

Helmet fit is most critical. An entire book could be written about proper helmet sizing and fitting. Follow your helmet manufacturer's guidelines and you will be OK. At the start of the year, lots of kids think their helmets are too tight and ask for a larger model. Sometimes they are right, but more often than not the snug fit is just how the helmet is intended to function. Encourage your player to give it time to adjust, but keep an open dialogue with them.

Pants are the other area where finding a perfect fit is difficult. Our organization provides black pants, used for both practices and games, with integrated pads. Keep an eye on how your kids' pants affect their movement. While they will complain about (or just flat out not fit in) pants that are too tight, loose pants are just as bad and while kids will generally try to make a go with them, they should be replaced as soon as possible.

Mouthguards are relatively inexpensive, and we provide each player with one and keep plenty of extras on hand for practices and games. If parents would like to buy one for their child, make sure they adhere to any rules your league may have regarding equipment. For example, our league stipulates the mouth guard's keeper strap be a different color than the facemask.

Individual equipment our organization does not provide includes cleats and gloves. Make sure parents understand limitations on these items before they spend a lot of money on them. For example, most leagues prohibit metal spikes and cleats exceeding a certain length. Leagues may also have regulations regarding wristbands, headbands, and other accessories.

Team equipment: While you may supplement with your own, it is not unreasonable to expect your organization to provide team equipment. Some valuable pieces can get quite expensive, but are manageable to a fiscally-responsible group.

Start with the items that are critical to ensuring your players' health and safety. First and foremost, make sure all players have access to water at all times during practices and games. This could mean a water "trough," large multi-gallon coolers or jugs, individualized water bottles, or something else altogether. Keep a helmet pump on hand to ensure optimal inflation for your helmets' protective bladders. Extra mouthguards and shoulder pad replacement pieces should also be readily available. In case of injury, keep ice packs, Ace bandages, and a fully-stocked First Aid kit available. Consider assigning a different coach to being the go-to person for each of these areas, as a handful of minor issues arise every day.

You can't play football without ... footballs. Plan on needing one for every four or five players on your team. Your organization should provide these, and while footballs are generally more durable and reusable than basketballs and baseballs, you should add several new balls each year. Make sure you are using the size mandated by your league's rules. Do not assume the labels on the box ("pop warner" or "junior" or "pee wee") correlate to the names used for age levels in your league. If possible, involve your quarterback or running backs in selection of these balls, and designate two as game balls. Keep a pump on hand to keep footballs properly inflated.

Other equipment you will need includes:
- Kicking tees, one for kickoffs and a block for extra points and the rare field goal try.
- Agility cones for marking playing fields and practice drills. Low-profile cones are better than the taller traditional traffic safety-style cones.
- Training chutes, or their less expensive cousin, carpets.
- Hand shields, half-rounds, and full-size dummies for blocking and tackling drills. I tease coaches in my organization that they are spoiled by the abundance of dummies at their disposal, but they have been very particular about the exact right dummy for each of their drills. You will find out over time what works best for your favorite drills.
- Large (at least 3 feet wide) dry erase board and markers.
- Video camera.
- Wrist coach wristbands (quantity depends on whether you huddle or not).
- Other optional items include agility ladder, high step agility trainer, snapper stick, tackle wheels.
- Perhaps most importantly, a whistle!

If you are coaching in an established organization, chances are many or most of these items will be immediately available to you. Take a day to find out, prioritize your equipment wish list, and work with your organization's leadership to acquire the most necessary items. Remember that in most cases equipment is usable for many years and can be shared among multiple teams at a time.

Before your first practice, take some time to familiarize yourself with the field and facility you will be using. Isn't a field just a field? Not exactly. During my years of coaching we have used a variety of different setups.

For several years our organization practiced in the outfield of a local baseball field, with three teams sharing two 50-yard fields. We were responsible for lining these fields, which carried expense associated with paint and volunteers' sanity as the painting machine malfunctioned. Our season started once baseball was finished, so we had no restrictions on practice times. An equipment shed and concession stand provided ample storage space. The field included a water source close enough to place a water trough near our practice areas. An outdoor bathroom was a short walk away. The park had lights that allowed us to practice later.

Several years ago this baseball field underwent upgrades and was unusable for football practice. Our local school district and varsity coach were gracious enough to allow us use of the high school practice fields directly adjacent to our elementary school. The location is more centrally located in our community and easier to reach for families traveling from our partner communities. We now have two fully-lined 100-yard fields at our disposal. But since we share fields with our high school team, we typically can not start until 5:30 p.m. Less storage space is available, and the water source is not feasible for us to keep running for an entire practice. The school allows us to use two of its restrooms.

Is one venue better than the other? Maybe for certain families' locations or situations, but overall? Not really. Our new location provides the opportunity to use a full-size field without the headache or expense associated with lining. The bathrooms are now close enough that a player can use them during the time elapsed in a typical water break. If the high school team practices past 5:30, we can start our warmups and other early-practice drills on another patch of grass. Lack of lights? Only an issue in the last few weeks of September and October, and you should probably be scaling back your practice times at that point in the season anyway.

The takeaway: lots of different venues can make for good practice fields. Make sure you understand any limitations they carry and plan your practices accordingly.

PART 3

Practice Planning

We are not going to lead this chapter with any maxims or cliches about the importance of practice. Everyone has heard those. Instead, let's consider two numbers. Assuming your season spans August and September and your team plays six games, you will spend:

- 70 hours practicing
- 9 hours playing games

Let's say you or your organization do not believe in practicing that much — that's fair. Even if you scale back to, say, 45-50 total hours of practice over the course of a season. You are still spending five times as many hours practicing than playing games. How you spend that time is vitally important to not only your team's success, but more importantly, the quality of your kids' experience and whether or not they continue to play football as they get older.

Watching youth football games, all too often it is painfully easy to identify teams that have not made the best use of their practice time. They have difficulty aligning correctly, struggle to execute a snap, see multiple players out of position on each play. It is hard to watch. Forget winning and losing. Those kids are not learning football. They might not stick around another year to start learning.

Here are some philosophies and concepts to make the most out of your team's practice time.

Plan

This seems obvious. But the number of youth sports coaches who begin practice without a well-articulated plan is disturbing. Practicing without a plan wastes time, wastes opportunities to teach kids, wastes chances to connect with kids. So create a plan for each practice. Make it as detailed as possible (we will share some ideas later in this chapter). Will you strictly stick to the minute-by-minute plan? Probably not. Will you need to be as detailed in your planning as you get into week 8 or 9? No. But establishing a detailed practice plan for the first month or so of practice will set your team on a path to making the best use of the time you spend together.

Communication

After establishing your practice plan, share it with your assistant coaches for feedback. Maybe you have too much time scheduled for a team session. There might be a drill that a coach does not understand. You may have forgotten a key phase to cover. Include your staff in the planning and you will hit the ground running.

Before the start of practice, summarize your goals for that day with your players. Cover any big-picture issues that need to be addressed. At the conclusion of practice summarize what you learned and what you need to work on the next time you get together. Ask your assistants if they have anything to add to the discussion.

Warning: Do not talk for the sake of talking! When you gather your team for a speech, you better have something of value and importance to share. A random Tuesday afternoon in September does not require Knute Rockne-level oratory. If every time your team circles around you a five-minute reflection on life follows, your kids will tune you out.

Music

Several years ago we started playing music during practice for our younger age group team. After several weeks, a coach from our older team remarked "I kinda wish we were down by you guys — you look like you're having fun!" And we were! No matter how well planned it might be, football practice can be a slog at times. At some point every kid will be waiting to take their next rep. Music can help make downtime pass a little quicker.

This past year music played another role in our game preparation. For the first time we went exclusively no-huddle, calling plays from the sideline off wristbands. While practicing this communication during team offense periods we blared music. It was tough to get the call in at times, and through this we discovered improvements to our system. When it came to the relative quiet of games we had zero issues with play calling communication. Note that we did not play music during teaching sessions. My voice could only take so much stress!

What type of music should you listen to? For starters, nothing with foul language or explicit content. Other than that, my preference is for anything up tempo: hip hop, metal, some classic rock. My fellow coaches are aware of my loathing for country music, so naturally they created a country playlist! Ask your kids for their music choices. All you need is a phone and one of the many affordable Bluetooth speakers on the market.

Some of my favorite memories of the past few seasons have involved music, from an impromptu dance-off among our players to, ahem, a coaches' dance-off. Give it a shot and see if it works for your team. And if you hold a coaches' dance-off, make sure no one is recording video!

Period Length

Recently I was re-reading a book on football drills published about 10 years ago, looking for ideas for next year. At the end of each drill's description was a recommended length. The vast majority of these drills were recommended to last — spit take — 30 minutes! At the risk of being one of those "kids these days" people, I defy you to show me a single activity (aside from video games) that any child can perform with effort and concentration for 30 consecutive minutes.

2018 I-S Pee Wee Practice Schedule

Thursday Aug 2nd HELMETS ONLY   Week 1-Day 2

Focus		Find the best 5 WR's			
Install		Need to try to move a step faster tonight			
Time	Period	Emphasis	All Players		
5:30	Team	Dynamic Warm Ups	Line Players up in 5 rows equal spacing. Steve will start this but eventually hand this over to Coach Tanner		
5:45	Team	Cadence & 3pt Stance	All on scrimmage line Cadence will be DOWN READY SET HUT (FEET, CHAIR, 5 FINGER EYE BALL, BACK FLAT, BUTT DOWN, ARM ON TABLE RELAXED, HEAD UP, EYES FORWARD, 6" STEP, ARMS OUT, HANDS IN W)		
5:50	Team	Water	1st break is 5 mins but we will shorten to 3 mins FOCUS on the slow pokes		
5:55	Team	Team Tackling Circuit			
		Break into 4 even groups of 5 Players-we use FEET SINK ARMS RIP SQUEEZE ROLL-5 mins each & will evolve next week. Matt & Jonah move to new stations			
		Superman Matt & Josh	Near Hip Near Shoulder Joe		
		Need 2 half round dummies, on knees (SINK & RIP) as they spring out make sure they are exploding with hip roll onto the bag and not using feet. This one seems simple but it is not if they are truly using just their hips to fling themselves out on the bag.	Start players walking at an angle to the cone-tackler near foot swoop break down tagging RB nearest hip with same hand as lead foot/shoulder combination R & L START SLOW so they get their foot work right. Make sure we are teaching so they will get in the correct tackling form.		
			I always try to keep their HEADS out of the tackle.		
		Firebird Roll Bob & Miles	Mike Tyson Uppercuts Steve & Jonah		
		Partner up players for the first week so the rookies learn quicker. 1 large circle, one on 1 knee foot centered to the standing player (EYES THROUGH THE THIGHS, FEET, SINK, ARMS, RIP SQUEEZE, & ROLL) Do both hips 3 reps each player. Make sure player is not fighting the tackler but not just falling down. FAST PACE! Uneven # coach might have to be the ball carrier.	Coach calls out the lead foot they will use for leverage. Players 5 yards back-run but once they are straddling the carpets folded in half they break down/swoop nearest foot attacking R or L hip. At the end of the bag they will UPPER CUT half rounds and drive for 5. Coaches needs to be offset a little & hold the bag straight out.		
6:15	Team	Carpets	5 rows half rounds & shields, drive for 5-Lay carpet down and to keep their feet wide at the front of the carpet we can also lay half rounds on the carpets to keep their feet out. Do a couple REPS from the back of carpet and meet them head on.		
6:25	Team	Water	Any Slow Pokes?		
	Offensive Indy's	OL (continue to rep potential centers)	QB/RB		QB/WR
		Coach Bob will pick Drills. Miles will help	Coach Steve will pick Drills. Josh will help		Coach Nick will pick Drills. Josh will help
6:30	OI	review stance and 1st & 2nd step	Review back first steps, hand placement, catching mechanics		
6:35	OI	step 1 and 2 with 5 yard duck chop	Two groups: 26/27 lead, 26/27 boot; 32/33 dive, 32 dive option right		
6:40	OI	intro drive block	Switch		
6:45	OI	Examples Sumo 1 on 1 Pass Protect	Introduce Pro plays - 27 lead, 34 crossbuck, 38 sweep; 28/29 pitch		
6:50	Team	Water	Poke a long Cassidy's?		
6:55	Team	Team Offense	Steve will add more plays. Set up and run just a defense just show Offense where the holes are. Zero contact.		
7:20	Team	Water	Who is last?		

Sample practice plan

Your kids will be far better served by limiting periods to no longer than 10 minutes. One exception is team periods — offense, defense, special teams — as those include a variety of actions within one period. Even then, consider breaking up your team periods into shorter segments, broken up by separate yet still valuable interludes. Here are some suggested lengths for potential activities you may use.

- Stretching/warmups: 5 minutes
- Tackle circuit: 15 minutes
- Blocking circuit: 10 minutes
- Offensive individuals: 15 minutes
- Defensive individuals: 10 minutes
- Team offense: 30 minutes
- Team defense: 20 minutes
- Special teams: 10 minutes

Note that several of these activities (tackle, blocking, individuals) should contain a variety of drills within them, so players will not be doing the same

Scott Tappa

thing for 10 minutes straight. As mentioned earlier, a longer activity like team offense can be broken up into one or two different actions, like kickoff or punt return.

Letting practices lapse into longer periods is the lazy way to coach, and results in disengaged players and coaches and sloppy work. Plan shorter, high-energy periods and stick to your plan.

Setting Up Your Season

Your first practice will almost certainly look different than your last. While teaching never stops, the nature of your teaching will change significantly over the course of the two-plus months you spend with your kids. Acknowledge the differing needs when setting up your season practice plans, paying extra attention to the first couple weeks.

Day one is as much of a learning day for you and your assistants as it is for your kids. For starters, you need to learn everyone's names! Chances are you know a good chunk of your roster without assistance, but if you and your

Number	First name	Nickname	Grade	Box Drill Time Coach Jim & Coach Mack		30 Yard Dash Time Coach Steve & Coach Mark		QB 4 throws @ 10 yards Coach Breen 25pts max for each throw				WR 4 catches @ 10 yards Coach Josh 25pts max for each catch				Postion Line or Hands
3	Liam	General	6	6.59	5.79	5.32	5.4	14	15	14	15	15	15	15	15	Line/X/Z
6	Noah	Ark	5	8.33	7.66	5.62	5.66	10	10	10	10	5	5	5	5	Line/X/Z
8	William	Billy	5	8.59	8.48	7.06	7.38	8	8	8	7	0	0	0	0	Line/X/Z
12	James	Jay	5	7.38	6.88	5.57	5.57	13	14	13	14	15	20	20	15	Line/X/Z
19	Logan	Snow	6	7.29	7.3	4.85	4.97	14	14	14	14	10	20	15	15	X/Z/CB/S
21	Ben	Bravo	6	8	6.98	5.06	5.19	8	8	8	8	10	5	5	0	Line/X/Z
26	Mason	Mase	6	9.36	8.46	5	5.09	14	15	15	15	20	20	20	20	Y/Z/CB
27	Elijah	E	5	7.59	8.03	4.6	4.85	15	18	18	19	20	20	20	20	Q/H/Y/S
28	Oliver	Cowboy	5	7.56	7.25	5.25	5.72	17	16	15	18	15	15	15	15	Line/Y/CB
31	Jacob	Jockey	5	5.93	5.73	5.29	5.34	10	10	10	10	15	15	15	20	Q/F/Z/NT/DE
32	Lucas	Luke	6	8.12	6.59	5.16	5.21	22	21	21	22	10	15	15	15	Line/X/DE
33	Michael	Mike	5	6.18	6.53	5.25	5.28	10	9	8	9	15	15	20	20	Q/F/LB/S
35	Alex	Big Al	6	6.76	6.48	4.97	5.12	15	15	15	15	15	10	15	10	H/LB/S/CB
37	Ethan	Bambino	6	6.45	6.23	4.84	4.94	14	15	15	15	15	15	15	20	Q/F/LB/NT
41	Daniel	Danny	6	6.98	6.26	4.78	4.85	16	17	16	17	20	20	20	20	Q/F/Z/S/DE
44	Matthew	Hawk	5	7.76	6.57	5.19	5.47	22	20	23	22	15	15	20	10	Line/CB/S/X
54	Aiden	Junior	5	6.73	5.82	4.87	4.94	12	12	12	12	5	5	10	5	Line/F/LB/DE/S
64	Henry	Hank	5	8.29	8.79	6.15	6.19	12	12	12	12	0	0	0	0	Line
76	Joseph	JJ	6	8.49	8.6	6.07	6.19	5	5	5	5	10	15	10	10	Line
82	Sam	Big Show	6	7.26	8.03	5.53	5.53	12	12	12	12	10	10	10	15	Line
93	Jackson	Jack	5	7.25	8.23	5.91	6.18	5	5	5	5	10	5	5	5	C/DT

Sample player evaluation

organization are doing a good job of recruiting, there will be fresh faces each August. The best tip is an oldie but goodie: write their names on a piece of tape and stick them to the front of their helmets. If you are using a Sharpie be sure to write on the tape before placing it on the helmet, as the ink can leak through.

    The other important learning experience for coaches is learning about your kids' abilities. More than likely you have a general sense about some of your kids' size, speed, and skills. But even the ones you have known since they were toddlers may have grown or gotten faster or developed better hands. Consider devoting about 30 minutes of your first practice to four testing stations: a 30- or 40-yard dash (or some other distance you think is a good measure of raw straight-ahead speed), a box or three-cone drill (or some other measure of side-to-side, change-of-direction agility), throwing, and catching. For the first two, give each kid two tries measured by a coach who ideally is an experienced timer. For the latter two, keep track of successful throws and catches and any other notes about form. Do not take for granted that your kids spend February watching the NFL Scouting Combine — you will need to explain even the 30-yard dash in detail. Compile your results in a centralized form, adding in positions you will try players at in the season's early going. In addition to being a good tool for positioning your players, this will also serve as an objective reference point for kids or parents who might complain about not playing a ball carrying position.

In the first couple practices, you will need to build time into your drills to explain each one in detail. Ideally you will have gone over most or all of these with your assistants, and a handful of your players who can jump in and demonstrate on the first day. But realistically both players and coaches will need explanation of each drill. If this means you spend less time actually performing the drill on day one, that's OK. Better to make sure everyone knows what to do and why they are doing it than to plunge in blindly and run half-baked drills in subsequent practices.

Your first two weeks of practices will also be influenced by the equipment and amount of hitting you are allowed. Our conference follows the rules set forth by our state's high school athletic association. The first two days of practice, players are limited to helmets and mouthguards, with only air, bags, and wrap contact allowed. On days three through five players may add shoulder pads, with the same restrictions on contact. Only after players have completed five days of acclimatization in limited equipment may they wear full pads (including pants) and engage in thud and full contact.

Given these parameters, consider weighting your first five practices more toward offense. While you can certainly run team and individual defensive drills, including certain elements of a tackling circuit, restrictions on contact make offense the more logical side of the ball to emphasize. Besides, in this coach's view, offense at the youth football level is more complicated and requires more reps to gain proficiency than defense.

One other consideration: will your team be scrimmaging? Historically our team has participated in a three-team scrimmage at the conclusion of the second week of practice. While we do not spend any time preparing for our scrimmage opposition, we make sure we are ready to run a set amount of base offensive plays and line up properly on defense. We typically do not spend much if any time on special teams in practices leading up to the scrimmage, and instead start working on those disciplines in the week leading up to our first game.

Two other considerations for practice leading up to your scrimmage and first game:

Review rules and penalties. Do not assume that every one of your players watches a lot of football and inherently knows the rules of the game. An effective way we have accomplished this is by taking a 10- or 15-minute break when practice is getting stale or monotonous and asking kids to name as many penalties as possible. You may be surprised that they can cover just about all frequently-called infractions.

Rehearse gameday procedures, from warmups to weigh-in, opening kickoff to standing on the sideline. We will go into more detail on gameday operations later, but consider incorporating as many of your Saturday activities into at least one practice before you go live. Do not take for granted that kids know where to stand when they are not in the game, where to assemble after they have been introduced, how to behave during halftime. Teaching these details ahead of time will make things go much smoother when emotions are high on the weekend.

Stretching/Warmups

Jumping jacks? No. Trunk rotations? Uh uh. Sitting down and stretching your ankles? Come on. Your team's time is precious, and you do not have enough of it to waste with static stretches from 1980s gym class. Use a dynamic warmup routine with your kids. Exactly what "dynamic warmup" means differs depending on what source you check, but the underlying theme is get your kids moving. Here is a suggested warmup routine for a team of 20-25 players.

- 30-yard single file jog
- Players separate into five equal lines
- Coach prompts different player to call out each action
- Players begin action when player in front of them reaches 5 yards
- 10-yard high knees
- 10-yard butt kicks
- 20-yard bounders
- 10-yard lunge and twist
- 10 pushups
- 10 situps/crunches/leg raises
- 10-yard backpedal (twice)
- 5-yard backpedal, 5-yard turn and sprint (twice)
- 10-yard carioca (twice)
- 10-yard and 20-yard sprints from three-point stance, using a variety of counts and cadences
- Water

You will need a coach to prompt these actions, and that coach will probably need these on a sheet of paper — it's a lot to remember! But encourage the kids to take ownership of warmups by finding their voice. This time is also a good time for coaches to greet kids and make small talk with them about their day.

Everyday Individual Drills

It may be tempting to rush into practicing plays or scrimmaging, but remember that teaching kids football is largely about fundamentals. No football skills are more fundamental than stance, blocking, and tackling.

Stance

Not all of your players will get in a three-point stance during any given season, but all should learn it. Overcoming a poor stance is difficult, and few children are naturally good at it. Common stance problems include feet spread too wide and staggered too far, legs crouched too much or not at all, too much or not enough weight on plant hand, and eyes looking down instead of straight ahead.

Here is a simple way to teach a player to properly assume a three-point stance: Start with your feet shoulder-width apart. Bend your knees, drop your butt and keep your legs straight in an athletic stance. Rest your elbows on your thighs, a position we call "chairs." Lean forward until your weight tips you, then stop your fall by throwing out your dominant arm. With with four or five fingers on the ground (not two, knuckles, or a fist), adjust your down hand to balance your weight in such a way that if someone were to slap it away, you would remain upright. Keeping your back straight, make sure your eyes are looking forward.

This is a significant challenge for most children, who lack the flexibility and leg and neck strength to properly assume this stance. Working on stance permeates most drills, and should be corrected and coached at each one. But devoting several minutes at the start of each practice to stance can go a long way toward getting your kids in the right position.

Tackling Circuit

Perhaps no area of youth football coaching has changed more in the past five years than tackling. Coaches who have been at it a while, or who draw from the experiences of their playing days, will need to unlearn principles like "put your helmet between their numbers" or "bite the ball." Driven by safety concerns, a rugby style popularized by Seattle Seahawks coach Pete Carroll, and adoption by USA Football, the "shoulder tackling system" has emerged as a leading method for teaching football tackling.

In addition, the last few years have seen a dramatic reduction of live practice hitting at all levels of football. In our youth organization, this has been influenced by a heightened awareness of concussion and other injury risks inherent with a collision sport like football. Subjecting your kids to a physical pounding every day at practice does not make sense for a variety of reasons. But with some thought and research, we have found you can teach tackling in a safer way without sacrificing toughness or effectiveness.

Proper coaching of the shoulder tackling technique requires a greater understanding than can be conveyed in a few paragraphs. I encourage you to check out the resources offered by USA Football and others. For purposes of this chapter on practice planning, here is the four-station daily tackling circuit we use. These drills are designed to train actual body movements and exaggerate them to establish muscle memory for proper shoulder tackling form.

Rip, squeeze, and roll: Players partner up, with one doing the tackling.

Tackler gets in athletic stance, with one foot between teammate's feet. Tackler proceeds to set his feet, sink his hips, shoot his arms back into gunfighter holster position, then rip, squeeze, and roll, taking his teammate to the ground. Tackler's head remains to the side. Tackled player is not fighting the tackle, providing minimal resistance as he falls to the ground. Each partner executes two reps rolling both right and left. Coach leads drill with "Feet! Sink! Arms! Rip, squeeze, and roll!" commands.

Near hip/near shoulder: An angle tackling circuit, players partner up 5 yards apart (progressing to 10 yards after kids get the hang of the drill), with one holding a hand shield. Partner with shield jogs forward at 45-degree angle, with tackler sprinting to meet him. Tackler buzzes feet, coming to balance and executes shoulder tackle without taking teammate to ground — keeping head to opposite side of shield carrier's path. The tackler's head is behind the tackle. For these first two drills, do your best to match players of similar sizes and abilities to limit mismatches.

Uppercuts: Coach holds half-round, players line up 10 yards away. On command, player sprints toward bag, buzzing his feet and coming to balance a yard or two before impact. Player sinks hips, then uppercuts half-round, wrapping and finishing for 5 yards after impact. Key coaching points are coming to balance (players can not simply run through the bag), sinking hips, and finishing.

Superman: At front of line, player gets on knees before half-round bag. On command, he explodes forward through his hips without using feet. This drill encourages hip explosion.

Each group of players spends 3-4 minutes at a station before rotating. There are subtle variations of these drills that we used throughout the season, and other changes we are considering for next. You may discover drills that rep individual tackling skills that make good substitutes for the ones listed above. Great! Bottom line: break tackling down into its component parts, break your players into small groups, and send them through a circuit of concise, high-rep drills that train those specific skills.

Blocking

As with tackling, there are a variety of ways to coach blocking, and the evolution has centered around emphasizing safety by keeping players' heads out of the action. We are not going to take a deep dive here into the details of blocking, but instead give you a simple method for organizing your daily blocking practice.

One word: Carpets. More words: you can use fortified carpet remnants to train a variety of blocking skills. Start by acquiring remnant carpet and cutting them into strips roughly 1 foot wide by 5 feet long. Reinforce their edges by wrapping the strips in duct tape. That's it — you now have yourself a training tool.

Carpets are intended as guides to ensure your players maintain the proper base they need when blocking. If the player's blocking footwork gets too narrow, he will step on the carpet. This is a similar training tool to chute boards used by offensive linemen at older levels. Only much cheaper!

When setting up the drill, lay out five carpets separated by enough space for players to assume normal offensive line splits. The player at the front of the line walks to the front and assumes the "chair" position described earlier. A lead coach calls out the cadence, with all players going down into their three-point stance in unison. The line then fires off in accordance with the snap count. Carpets are a great time to continue working on players' stance, and a perfect time to work on snap count discipline without jumps disrupting the rest of the team's flow.

Who do the blockers fire off at? We have used two different options: a coach holding a hand shield and another similarly-matched player. Each has its advantages. A coach can properly regulate the amount of resistance the blocker feels, correct technique in real time, and motivate. Yet a teammate is clearly the better representation of the type of body your kid will be blocking in a game. Be sure to vary the positioning of the coach or teammate from head up (best for linemen and tight ends) to 3-4 yards back (best for guards, fullbacks, and receivers).

While carpets are a great way to isolate and train blocking technique, it should not be the only time during daily practice when these skills are worked. Obviously your offensive line will work at this extensively, but backs and receivers should as well. In both cases the transition from carpets to position groups drills should be a step further in the game-like blocking scenario: fullbacks lead blocking through a specific hole, guards executing a double team, etc.

Individual Drills

Referred to in shorthand as "indys," position drills are an essential part of daily practice. As the name implies, indys work position-specific skills, but also begin moving players toward their roles on any given play. For example: a halfback practices footwork, hand placement, ball security, and vision on air while executing his assignment on 26 Lead. Two important things to remember regarding indys:

1. As a season progresses, your practices become shorter and games make clear what your team needs to emphasize, there will be a temptation to cut indy time in favor of team sessions. Resist that urge. As a youth football coach, your priority is teaching fundamentals and skills, and that is best accomplished in small group environments. If anything, you should devote more time to indys as the season progresses. Do not get lazy with this critical aspect of practice planning.

2. Instruction is best accomplished in small groups. If you are fortunate enough to have five or six assistant coaches, use every single one of them during indys. Break kids into smaller groups by specific position (for example, break offensive linemen into tackles and guards), by ability or by age group (for example, a backfield comprised of fourth graders and a backfield comprised of third graders). This will allow each player to get maximum reps and accelerate their development.

While the name "individual" drills may imply a single player performing the action, it more accurately applies to individual position groups. How you define these position groups depends on the size of your team and the number of coaches at your disposal to run drills. Also, some players like centers or tight ends may end up splitting time between two position groups during indys. It takes a fair amount of planning and coordination but is vital to ensure your kids are repping appropriate skills.

What follows is a suggested approach to running offensive and defensive indys for a team of 20-25 players with five or six total coaches, running 10-15 minutes. As noted earlier in this book, we will not go into detail about particular drills — there are myriad sources for these ideas — but instead give organizational ideas.

Offensive Indys

Offensive line: Assuming your team has already spent time repping blocking on carpets, indys are when you connect specific blocks to specific plays. Start by separating into two groups: tackles and tight ends, and guards. Given our team's plays and our league's defensive rules, guards will work on double teams and finding linebackers 3 yards off the line of scrimmage, while tackles and tight ends will block defenders head up. Note that during the first part of offensive indys centers will be with backs and receivers working on snaps.

After five minutes separate, bring all linemen together and rep blocking individual run plays. In order to maximize reps, the emphasis should be on first steps and fits. There is no need for these reps to last more than 5 seconds. Ideally you will have enough linemen to create an entire defensive front, but if not you can fill in the gaps with coaches holding hand shields or half rounds.

Finally, you will want to spend a few minutes on pass blocking. How much time you devote to this skill depends on how much your offense passes. Start with the entire unit repping your technique for pass blocking footwork, then progress to competitive reps in which a live group protects a coach or tackling dummy for a set amount of time (3 seconds is a good rule of thumb). Do your best to match up players of similar size and ability for these reps and create incentives to maximize the drills' competitiveness. Be sure to recall your centers to take part in the latter half of offensive line indys.

Backs/receivers: If possible aim to have two groups running concurrently, each with a center executing snaps. You can never get your centers enough practice snapping! Have each group run through the actions of your base run plays: leads, dives, tosses/sweeps, jet sweeps, crossbucks. The most critical part of this session is speed: an accurate center snap, clean quarterback catch and footwork, clean footwork and hand placement by backs. Use a coach to add an element to the end of each run: knock the ball carrier with a hand shield to simulate running between the tackles, simulate an approaching safety to force the ball carrier to make a cut, etc.

One coach's opinion: Try to avoid drills that train only one skill like cutting or ball security and have no tie to game-like motions. Aim to incorporate the former with the latter for maximum efficiency. You may find videos of college or professional teams training one of these specific skills, and they are great, but remember that you have a lot less practice time than those guys, and your kids also need to learn defense.

Roughly two-thirds of the way through your offensive indy period, transition to passing. If your tight ends have been working with the offensive line, call them over. At the same time, release your centers to get work in with the line — coaches can simulate the snap for these reps, as can other players between reps. As with running plays, try to get two groups going at once, each using two quality footballs to minimize the wait between reps. Pay attention to detail during this session. Insist your receivers catch with their hands, not their body. Make sure routes are run precisely and not rounded off. If your play design calls for the quarterback to roll out, make sure he does it here.

At the beginning of the year, when you have more practice time and are still learning about your kids' abilities, all backs and receivers should run through every run play and pass route. As the season progresses and practice time becomes more precious, optimize your indy time by focusing kids on the runs and routes they will most likely be performing in a game.

Defensive Indys

In my opinion, you do not have to devote quite as much time to defensive indys as you do to offensive. To be clear my focus on the offensive side of the ball influences my thinking here. But realistically, a good youth football defense is far simpler schematically than even a basic offense, so most of your work in defensive indys can be focused on straight skill development.

Assuming you address tackling with the circuit described earlier or something similar, devoting 10-15 minutes to defensive indys should be sufficient. Separate your kids into defensive tackles/nose tackles, defensive ends, linebackers, and defensive backs. If coaching resources are limited, combining linebackers and defensive backs makes sense. While their priorities and assignments will be different, their physical actions will be more similar than any two position groups.

Team Sessions

At the beginning of the season, your team sessions will likely include a lot of time practicing "on air," or 11 players operating without a opposition. This is a cleaner environment for installing plays and concepts than trying to move 22 players around. If you have at least 22 players and enough coaches to properly manage the session, consider going with two separate groups during these periods. Twice the reps!

As the season progresses and your kids get a good handle on things, you will likely phase out on air reps in favor of 11-on-11 reps. This does not mean instruction stops. It just takes on a different form, as your scout defense or offense reveals flaws in your play design or execution.

A mistake to avoid: grinding activity to a halt to make a coaching point to a single player. While it is your obligation to diagnose and correct mistakes your players make, doing so while 20 other kids stand around waiting is not an efficient use of time. Try coaching on the run, or communicating with a player between reps while the rest of the team transitions to the next rep. If you need longer to make a point, do so during a water break, after practice, or the next practice during indys. It can be challenging, but if you are concise and use a common language, coaching on the run is huge time maximizer.

The concept of team sessions is straightforward enough. But remember: don't use it as a substitute for small-group work because you are too lazy to plan and coordinate it. Don't let team sessions drag on for long periods of time — break them up into smaller chunks separated by indys or special teams drills.

Tempo

Keeping speeches to a minimum. Short periods. Music. Small groups. Coaching on the run. All of these play a role in creating a high-tempo practice environment that maximizes the time you spend with your kids.

There has been no shortage of words written about typical kids' attention spans. While some of it may be overblown, we have also seen plenty of youth football players kicking at the grass with their spikes, staring at nearby playground shenanigans, or causing general mischief while waiting for their next turn in line. Rather than simply complain about it and yell at kids, do everything in your power to create a practice environment with minimal opportunity for young minds to wander. Keeping the proceedings moving at a brisk pace takes planning, energy, and discipline, but it is well within your power.

Conditioning

A positive byproduct of up-tempo practices is the reduced need for dedicated conditioning periods. To be clear, this is not to say that conditioning is unimportant to a football team. "Fatigue makes cowards of us all," "games are won or lost in the fourth quarter" — right, we get it. But if you design your practices to move along at an up-tempo pace in which players are rarely stationary for extended periods of time, they will be conditioning the whole time.

Think about it this way: let's say your team practices 25 times over the course of a season. You devote the last 10 minutes of practice every day to conditioning drills that involve nothing but running and other activities unrelated to football skills. By the time you are done, your kids will have spent more than four hours just running! That might be valuable for a cross country team, but football requires far more skill and teamwork, and those four hours can be better spent honing technique and strategies. Additionally, when kids know they will be ending practice with conditioning, they will conserve energy during other drills throughout the evening, and lessen the positive impact of those sessions. Bottom line: conditioning is important, but with some foresight and planning you can make it a part of everything your team does, not just a dreaded end-of-practice ritual.

(Caveat: Our kids have always loved ending practice with relays. Go figure)

Talk it Up

If you are the type of person who volunteers to coach a youth football team, chances are you would not qualify as a full-on introvert. One of the benefits of coaching is making new friends, something that does not always come easily in adulthood. You spend a lot of time with your fellow coaches, so there are plenty of opportunities to talk about the NFL, hunting, cars, grilling, music, your local high school team, movies, and other things guys talk about. Oh, and your team of course!

That is all well and good, and we encourage that. I've made some great friends through coaching and would not trade that for anything. But never lose sight of who you are there for: the kids.

These aren't just X's and O's on a dry erase board, they are little human beings who have complex feelings and emotions. Some may be the happy-go-lucky type who you never worry about. Others may come from a troubled home and struggle to get to practice on time. Some may be physically advanced and seemingly have football figured out, but might be struggling with the emotional side of athletics. Others may be struggling in school, or wondering why their parents signed them up for a sport that does not really interest them.

They are all your kids, and they need you and your assistants. Take time every day to talk personally with at least one of your players before practice, between drills, after practice. Even if they are shy, they will appreciate the individual attention. Those interactions will be what they remember years from now when they think back on their football experience.

PART 4

Offense

Back in high school I would draw football plays in my notebook for hours on end. In college my friends and I would draw 7-on-7 plays for our flag football game that week. When playing Madden or Tecmo Bowl, I never really cared about controlling the players after the snap — scrolling through the menu of plays and selecting the right one was the most important thing.

None of these things prepared me for coaching a youth football offense. The plays you see on Sunday, on Xbox, or on Twitter are by and large not good fits for 8- and 9-year-olds who are smaller, slower, and weaker-armed. Physical limitations aside, youth football players have a fraction of the practice time to perfect techniques and schemes.

That said, if you love offensive football, are creative and realistic, and put in the work, you can create and coordinate a youth football offense that is sound, effective, and fun.

Later I will share diagrams of some basic plays to help get you going if you do not know where to start. They should not be misconstrued as a "system," but instead are a variety of concepts that have worked. What follows are general philosophies on designing and running a youth football offense. Remember that in our conference, defensive tackles are required to line up head up on offensive tackles, nose tackles head up on centers; defensive ends must line up beyond the outside shoulder of tight ends or the spot tight ends would ordinarily line up; linebackers and defensive backs must line up at least 3 yards off the line of scrimmage (except inside their own 10-yard line); no more than three linebackers may line up in the box (the area between the outside shoulder of each offensive tackle); and no blitzing is allowed.

Before diving in, consider this overarching philosophy: whatever you decide to do offensively, from positioning players to system or play type to tempo to play calling, do it with the intention of competing with and succeeding against the best teams in your league. There are plenty of ways for a youth football offense to gain yards and score points by "out-athleting" teams, and you will quickly learn what those are. Resist the urge to take the easy way out by constantly running sweeps and pitches. Commit to developing players and schemes that will succeed against well-coached, top-flight athletes.

Offensive Systems

There is no shortage of potential offenses for your youth football team to run. A Google search of "football offenses" returns 15.2 million results in under a second! There are not quite that many offensive systems available, but as someone with more than a passing interest in football you can probably name quite a few off the top of your head. Wing-T. Run-and-shoot. Pro-style. West

Coast. Pistol. Air Raid. Triple option. Spread. Where to start?

Here's a suggestion: have a conversation with your high school coach and see if he has any thoughts or preferences. Your coach may insist or strongly prefer you run some form of the offense teams run at all age levels in your local program. Start training kids at an early age in the concepts, terminology, and techniques they will be using throughout their years in the program. Conversely, your high school coach may not have a strong preference what you run, realizing that many of the schemes and actions run by 17-year-olds are beyond the capabilities of a typical 10-year-old with a fraction of the practice time. He just wants your kids to learn fundamentals, have fun, and continue playing when they reach high school. There are ways to integrate concepts used by your high school team into your youth offense, even if you choose not to go all the way in.

So what system should you use? Do you even need a system, or will a collection of proven plays suffice? In my experience, youth football teams generally run no more than 10-12 distinct plays (double that number if you include versions of each play going both right and left) that use 3-5 different formations. Oftentimes these plays clearly complement or build upon each other (more on that later). Whether or not this can constitute a "system" might just be a matter of semantics or branding. With teams running an average of 35-40 offensive plays per game, do you really need more than that?

It is a question you need to consider before the season, during the preseason, and every week of the season. The trick is to keep your active playbook simple and limited enough to get sufficient reps during your limited practice times — with kids rotating in and out at many positions — without being too simple to succeed against the best defenses on your schedule.

Over the course of my first six years of coaching, our offense lined up with two running backs about 90 percent of the time, split between I and Pro formations; single-back Trips or Double Wing 5-10 percent of the time; and one-off special formations a handful of plays per season. Out of those alignments we ran fairly standard plays: halfback off-tackle, fullback dive, halfback or quarterback sweep, crossbuck, bootleg, counter, option, tight end pass, split receiver vertical pass, and bubble screen (See Chapter 10 for diagrams of these plays). In recent years we have begun to add more modern concepts that reflect what is happening at the high school and higher levels, and that has been both fun and effective. But those 10-12 bread and butter plays served us well.

Whatever number of plays you decide your offense needs, be sure to allocate enough practice time to rep each sufficiently. Do not show up on Saturday and call plays your kids have only run once or twice in their lives. Consider that the more plays you install and rep, the more time you will need for team offense, which leads to less time to teach your kids defense, special teams, and all of the individual skills that go into football.

Complementary Plays

Let's say you aim for 10-12 bread and butter plays, leaving room for 5-6 additional one-off plays with specialized formations or actions. You can break those base plays down even further into 5-6 base plays that are complementary and build off each other with counters. This allows you to simplify the formations and actions you teach without sacrificing playbook diversity. For instance:

- 27 Lead sets up 27 Bootleg
- 32 Dive sets up 32 Dive Fake Option Right
- 47 Jet Sweep sets up 47 Jet Fake Option Right

What is basically three offensive play concepts — halfback lead, fullback dive, wingback jet sweep — becomes six plays. If you want, you can design these to go both right and left, so it is really 12 plays. The more you can structure your offense to include base plays with one or more complementary counters, and not rely on standalone one-off plays, the better.

Passing

Passing in youth football is difficult. You may have kids with good arms who excel as baseball players, but throwing a football while wearing shoulder pads and other required equipment is tough for most youngsters. In addition, most kids are not natural pass catchers or route runners — they tend to float and use their bodies to catch the ball, which may work just fine on the playground at recess but is problematic in an organized tackle football game.

While passing may be difficult it is not impossible. In our most recent season our team passed roughly 30 percent of the time, throwing as many as 20 passes in a single game. This was by far the most any team I have been associated with has passed, but it went well and helped get a variety of different kids touches. The running game will undoubtedly be the foundation of any youth football offense, but if you would like to incorporate passing consider these three concepts.

1. Do not ask your quarterback to stand in the pocket on a regular basis. Two reasons: many kids who end up playing quarterback are shorter than the linemen who block for them, and pass blocking is a difficult skill that takes far more practice time than you will be able to devote to a skill your kids do not use much. If you have a tall, rocket-armed kid and stout line, awesome, you can run passing plays out of the pocket. If not, rather than asking your quarterback to

throw blindly, unable to step into a throw while feeling intense pressure from the opposing front, design plays for the quarterback to roll out 3-5 steps. He will see the field better and be exposed to less potential pass rushers.

2. Do not design pass plays with three or four potential receivers and ask your quarterback to go through a progression. On a typical play your quarterback will have time to check two receivers maximum. If neither is open, tuck it and run.

3. Do not design pass plays that ask receivers to run straight routes and catch passes over their shoulders. It is really hard! Quarterbacks will struggle to hit their teammate in stride. Even if they do, receivers struggle to execute the body control to make that catch as intended; more likely, at some point they will turn around and start backpedaling, leaving them in poor position to catch even a perfectly-thrown pass. Help your receivers out by drawing pass routes directing them to make 90- or 45- degree breaks, getting their head and shoulders turned back toward their quarterback. If you do need to run a straight vertical route, specify which of the receiver's shoulders (inside or outside) the quarterback should target.

An important postscript to these passing thoughts: all of these revelations came from discussions with our players. Our quarterback suggested adding a rollout to our base tight end pass play. Our tight end suggested turning the primary route on that play from a go route to a corner. Your eyes can tell you a lot about what your kids can or can not handle, but so can they. Do not underestimate your kids' football intelligence. Maintain a dialogue with them about all aspects of your team and you might be surprised at how much better their thoughts and suggestions can make your entire operation.

The Snap

Nothing is more important than a successful snap. In my opinion, the leading cause of ineffective youth football offense is not poor play design, subpar line play, or generally weaker athletes. It is slow execution, and the leading cause of slow execution is inconsistent center-quarterback exchange.

During your first practice, give any kid who wants to try the opportunity to snap. Your group of potentials will be largely the kids identified as offensive linemen but do not hesitate to give your backs a shot at it if they express interest. It is that important! As you go through the process of identifying centers, keep in mind any weight limit rules your league has in place. In our conference, any player heavier than 108 pounds (younger level) or 138 pounds (older level) is limited to playing defensive tackle, offensive tackle, or center. If you have a large number of these restricted players on your roster, it is in your best interest for one of these kids to become your center.

Aim to narrow your pool of potential centers to two or three players by the end of the first week of practice. That will provide enough depth at the position to deal with injuries, absences, or ineffectiveness while not tying too many players to one position. Sticking with the same starter and backup throughout the season is preferable, but do not be afraid to make a switch if a kid struggles with the snap, blocking, or remembering your count or cadence.

The center-quarterback exchange can not be repped enough in practice, before games, and during games. At practice, put a ball in your centers' hands in as many different situations as makes logistical sense. Working on stance. During carpet blocking drills. Working with backs and receivers in offensive indys. Team offense periods. Maximize the number of snaps your centers and quarterbacks rep in practice and you will see the payoff on game days.

Regarding shotgun vs. under-center: this depends on your play design. After years of going with both, this past year our team used shotgun for all but one of our offensive plays during the course of the season. Why? Our line was on the smaller side, we were looking to pass more, and we were installing a read option package. Shotgun snaps lent themselves to these considerations more than under-center.

If you have a large offensive line and plan on pounding the rock 95 percent of the time, or if you play in an area where it regularly rains, or if you just can not find a center to execute the shotgun snap, then under-center might be better for your team. In hindsight, we should have devoted more practice reps to under-center snaps, in the event that we needed them situationally during the course of the season. My advice: choose the type of snap you will use on the majority of your plays and rep the heck out of it, but work in the other one for a few minutes every week.

Cadence and Count

These corollaries to the snap may seem trivial. They are anything but. Our teams have used three basic cadences over the years.

- "Down, set, hut!" The simplest cadence, with three elements. To go on two, three, or more, just add more "huts." This cadence is best for quick counts, like going on "set."
- "Blue 42, Blue 42, set, hut!" Four elements, and the repetitive first two can serve to share information about the defense, an adjustment to the play, or something else.
- "Down ... ready, set, hut." We have used this the last couple years without issue. Four elements, and the drawn-out "down" is good for everyone getting set correctly. Tougher to go on "set" but not hard to go

on "ready." The rhythm of this cadence is favorable for plays that use motion.

Whatever cadence you use, teach it on the first day of practice and do not change during the course of the season. Use it in all offensive individual and team drills, warmups, and stance/get-off work. Conversely, during defensive drills mix up cadences. You can not expect your opponents to use the same as you.

Regarding snap count: I prefer going on one as often as possible. There will be times we go on two or three, but I prefer to keep it simple. During your first few weeks of practice, you have a million things to teach your players. On offense alone you are installing plays, formations, position names, and the techniques and movements that go with each. These are much easier for a kid to remember when they are not also trying to remember the snap count. When we are repping indys, full team on air, or full team vs. scout, I would rather focus on teaching our players to run things correctly than stopping every minute or so to get frustrated with the one or two kids who inevitably forget the count and jump offside.

To be clear: having the ability to stay disciplined and go on two or three is a great thing to have in your back pocket for a situation where 5 free yards would come in handy. Also, you need to work against multiple-count cadences on defense, as your opponents will probably not use the same snap count every play. Rep multiple-count cadences during the stance/get-off/sprint portion of your warmup, or during defensive line indys. Use multiple-count cadences with your scout team offense when repping team defense — the scout players love going on two or three (or four, or silent count for that matter), and take great pride in not jumping.

While learning plays, though, keep your snap count simple. It is more important to teach your players how to play football than it is to teach them how to count.

Blocking

When designing plays for your team, keep in mind one underlying principle: all 11 defenders need to be accounted for. Whether with blocks, fakes, formations or other methods, consider how every player on the opposing defense might stop your play and build in a means for negating that. Because nothing ever goes perfectly according to plan, on most plays at least one of the 11 defenders will derail your play before its best possible conclusion, but the more of those players accounted for on the front end, the less likely that is to happen.

The most common method of neutralizing defenders is blocking. Here are some blocking-related thoughts, not necessarily technique but as it pertains to play design.

Most big plays in youth football are runs around the end. Give your fastest kid the ball and tell him to outrun everyone to the corner, right? Putting on your defensive coordinator hat for a moment, it makes sense to put your best athletes at defensive end, right? While studs can reside at any position on defense, we have seen some monster defensive ends over the years that have almost single-handedly disrupted opposing offenses. Do your best to limit this possibility by double teaming the playside defensive end on running plays. Most often this will happen with a tight end and wingback or fullback. And it must be a solid double team, not just two guys hoping to get in the end's way. Be sure your blockers get hip to hip and box him in, maintaining their blocks until the whistle. The best defensive ends are strong, athletic and aware enough to peel off and chase a play down.

At the opposite end of the spectrum, most of our plays are designed to leave one defender unblocked. It is the ball carrier's responsibility to make that would-be tackler miss with a juke, stiff-arm, or pure speed. The unblocked defender will not be a player presumed to be one of the other team's stud athletes, a middle linebacker or defensive end, so it should be within your backs' capabilities. If your backs do not have the skills or athleticism to beat one defender, you will need to adjust your blocking scheme to account for all potential playside tacklers. The downside here is you will be taking resources away from slowing the defense's best players. But don't be stubborn and leave your kids out to dry asking them to do things they are not physically equipped to do.

Related to this point, the defender you task your ball carrier with beating will often be a cornerback. If you follow this philosophy, you will not need to split a player out in a traditional wide receiver alignment. Keep that player in closer to the line to provide additional numbers blocking against the defense's stronger tacklers. This is doubly true of receivers or wingbacks situated opposite the play side. If you are running off tackle right, there is no point in splitting a receiver out 10 yards to the left. Keep him attached to the line and assign him to blocking the weakside defensive end, which either provides a better backside seal or allows an additional blocker to engage linebackers.

To be sure, there are times when we split a receiver wide and ask him to stalk block a defensive back. You might find yourself designing plays where this is a critical function. Just don't fall in the trap of splitting a receiver out wide because that is what you are used to seeing on Saturdays and Sundays. Make sure all 11 of your kids are contributing on every play.

If you coach a non-select, everybody-plays team that competes in a league with minimum play rules for all players, you will need to find spots for smaller, less experienced and less physically mature kids can contribute. One of the common spots we have found — in a conference where defenses are required to play odd-man fronts with defensive linemen head up on their offensive counterparts — is at guard. That is not to say you will never put plus athletes at guard — over the years we have had many kids do a fantastic job at this position and contribute positively to our offensive success. But when designing blocking schemes, do not expect your guards to be pulling and performing other advanced techniques seen by linemen at older levels.

The most common run blocking assignments for guards are engaging a linebacker, double teaming the nose tackle or a defensive tackle, or an initial double team to neutralize a tackle before climbing to a linebacker. You may find yourself changing this approach from game to game depending on your opponent. Devote one coach to watching guard play closely during practice and games and provide those players with immediate feedback. Getting positive play from your guards can be the difference between having a good offense and a great offense.

Do not forget to rep pass blocking in practice. Even if you run 90 percent of the time, your team will almost certainly throw at some point or another. Run blocking and pass blocking are vastly different skills and need to be trained as such. Be sure to include your backs in these reps, as they will need practice identifying the correct pass rusher to pick up. Review and reinforce ineligible player downfield rules with your line. Some officials will be lenient, but sometimes linemen wander so far downfield on passing plays that it has to be flagged.

About 90 percent of people are right-handed, which means that your quarterback will probably throw with his right hand, be more comfortable running to his right, etc. Youth football offenses tend to be run-dominant and do not use many five- or seven-step drops straight back in the pocket. This de-emphasizes the need to protect the quarterback's blind side. Given this, whether consciously or not you will likely default to calling more plays to your offense's right-hand side. By extension you will also probably put your best lineman at right tackle. Taking this one step further, smart defensive coordinators will place their best linemen at left defensive tackle. Consider breaking this tendency by making your offense left-handed, regardless of which arm your quarterback uses to throw. You should still run plays to both sides of the field; hash marks on the fields you will play on are wide enough that you will not want to beat your head running to the short side. But consider this minor positional tweak to gain an advantage in the run game.

There are few things more important to good offensive football than effective blocking. Celebrate your blockers and make sure they know that even if they are not the ones breaking off long runs and scoring touchdowns, their contributions are absolutely vital to the team's success. They should also know that their block need not end in a defender pancaked on the grass in order to be effective. If your line comes off the ball quick and low, takes the proper first step, fits reasonably well, and maintains their blocks to the whistle, they are all-stars. Easier said than done, but keep in mind that you do not need dominant beasts along your line to field an effective, explosive offense.

Splits

If reading 600 words about the importance of line splits is not your cup of tea, by all means skip this section. Wait, don't — splits are really important! This seemingly minor detail could make a world of difference in your running game.

During my first year coaching, we scrimmaged several of the stronger teams in our conference after two weeks of practice. The results were troubling. Play after play was stuffed by opposing defensive linemen and we struggled to generate anything positive between the tackles. Before our first game we tightened our line splits from fingertip-to-fingertip to fingertip-to-shoulder. Over the course of that season we had pockets of offensive success, but it typically came with outside runs and against physically weaker opponents. During your time coaching you will almost certainly encounter times when you struggle to block the opponent's front seven or eight players. Resist the urge to address this by tightening your line splits.

The rules of the conference in which our teams compete restrict line splits to no more than fingertip-to-fingertip, and that is how we align our center, guards, tackles, and tight ends. The reason is simple: to create the widest possible running lanes for our backs. My younger son is 10 years old, slightly above average size. His arms are about 24 inches long. Assuming our linemen are a similar size, with fingertip splits our holes at the snap will be 4 feet wide. With two tight ends attached to the line, that is 24 feet of holes available for our run game.

Take the opposite end of the spectrum, fingertip-to-shoulder splits. Using simple math, we know that holes are now just 2 feet wide, and we have just 12 feet of total holes to work with from tight end to tight end. That is a huge difference! In addition to smaller running lanes, tighter splits naturally bring more defenders closer to the ball.

To be sure, tight splits work effectively in certain situations. They lend themselves well to plays and systems based on misdirection and deception. Tight splits are also a solid strategy for teams that may not feature much speed but hold a significant size advantage over their opponents. There is no simpler way to move the football than with brute force, pounding it up the gut 3 or 4 yards at a time.

But if your inclination is to tighten splits to account for struggles blocking, think twice and consider different methods of addressing the problem. Obviously you continue to work with linemen on their skills and techniques, but there are ways your scheme can help your blockers. Build in double teams to help struggling linemen. Overload a formation to create playside numbers advantages. Or leave defenders unblocked and read them instead.

Be vigilant about insisting your linemen align with the widest splits allowable. If you have watched a youth football game you have likely seen linemen approach the line of scrimmage with their arms outstretched to help guide their alignments. Even with this easy-to-use physical aid, linemen still align improperly — a lot! The most common mistake is arms bent at the elbows, which if allowed cuts down on the space between blockers by a foot or more. The amateur psychiatrist in me thinks that this is a combination of sloppiness and kids' natural inclination to crave being part of a group and not isolated on an island, where their potential mistakes are easier to spot. But if you choose to employ wide splits, reinforce it in everything you do: warmups, offensive indys, team offense — everything. Paired properly with a scheme that takes advantage of the resulting running lanes, wide splits will create a better environment for your team to run between the tackles.

A final splits-related note: when calling plays, you need to be disciplined enough to accept plays that yield 3, 4, 5 yards at a time. Do not fall into a trap of calling tosses and sweeps to your fastest back repeatedly. This may work against weaker opponents but almost certainly will not against stronger ones. Fullback dives for 3 yards are beautiful!

Positioning Your Players

It goes without saying that which of your kids play certain positions will depend on their abilities and the offense you run. If you run 100 percent of the time, you will not need a quarterback with a strong arm. If you play with four receivers most snaps, you may not need a traditional fullback. You will figure this out as time goes on. As you do, be sure to rep at least three different kids at each ball carrying or receiving spot. Further, make it a priority to get as many of those kids as possible game reps and touches.

It is unrealistic that over the course of a six-game season you will be able to get all of your kids touches. That needs to be made clear to your players and their parents at the start of the season. But the more kids you can involve in a game in this fashion, the better. Some youngsters are just linemen, and some want nothing to do with the pressure that comes with carrying the ball and getting tackled. Most do, though, and the more you can satisfy their urge for a carry or catch here and then, the more likely they will remain excited about the part of football some find mundane.

To Huddle or Not to Huddle

There is a certain romance associated with the football huddle. Close your eyes and you can see the quarterback making a fiery speech or cracking a joke, propelling his team to the winning score.

Spoiler alert: this isn't Hollywood, and you don't need to huddle.

Huddling on offense is not wrong, per se. Teams have huddled for years with great success, and will for years to come. There is something to be said for gathering all 11 players, getting their marching orders straight, then going into battle as a unit. My assertion is that ditching the huddle is a move worth making for a variety of reasons, strategic and otherwise. The overwhelming reason is this: more reps and more plays.

In the five seasons leading up to the most previous one, using a traditional huddle and pace, our teams averaged around 35 offensive plays per game, with a high of 38 and a low of 31. During the most recently-completed season we went no-huddle and operated at a faster pace, and averaged 43 plays per game. Two times we ran 57 plays in a game. While our no-huddle sample size is small, it does not seem unreasonable to suggest that by ditching the huddle a team can run 8-10 more offensive plays per game. Over the course of a six-game season, that's 50-60 additional plays. That's 50-60 more opportunities to get different kids game reps at ball handling spots. That is important in their short-term enjoyment and long-term participation in football.

The real benefit of going no-huddle is in practice. By committing to an up-tempo pace during team offense periods, your team can get up to twice as many reps as they would by practicing at a more deliberate pace. During the past two seasons we have recorded video of our team sessions, a practice I highly recommend for a variety of reasons (more on that later). We found that we averaged one play every 30 seconds when not huddling, compared to a play every 60 seconds when huddling. Part of that difference was the result of a concerted effort to coach on the run and not slow the pace for corrections at the end of every play.

Let's do some math (my favorite!). Last chapter we assumed 25 practices over the course of a season. Say you average 30 minutes per day in some form of team offense. This is on the high end, but makes for a nice, round number. Moving at a slower pace, you will run 750 plays. Using a fast-paced no-huddle tempo, you will run 1,500 plays. Even a more conservative figure, say averaging 20 minutes of team offense per practice, yields a difference of 500 plays vs. 1,000.

That is huge! With all those extra practice reps you can build kids' experience at different positions, expand your playbook, or just get lots better at your more limited playbook.

If you decide no-huddle is for you, the first critical step is choosing a communication system. There are plenty of options out there, hand signals and oversized boards among them. We decided to go with wristbands on every player. There are many sizes available, and after measuring our kids' arms we went with wristbands with a 2-¼ by 3-¾-inch window opening. A single-window band will suffice, as you should not have so many plays you need more than one.

For the card insert, we created in Excel a template with 11 rows and three columns (see page 84). This meant we could list 33 plays on our wristbands for a given practice or game. Each row had a distinct color, and each column a distinct number. We established color-number protocols that would direct each player to a play on the wristband. Pretty simple. Surprisingly, we did not change much of this over the course of the season. The one exception came when we created position-specific cards for our guards, some of whom were struggling

	1	2	3
Orange	Strong Left 27 Stretch	Strong Right 34 Counter	Strong Left Mesh
Yellow	Strong Right 26 Stretch	Pro Right 27 Stretch	Strong Right Mesh
Green	Strong Right 27 Boot	Trips Right Bubble	Strong Left Levels
Red	Strong Left 26 Boot	Trips Right Bubble and Go	Strong Right Levels
White	Strong Right 28 Sweep	Pro Right 38 Sweep	Slots Quick
Blue	Strong Left 29 Sweep	Pro Right 18 Sweep	Slots Two Go
Purple	Strong Left QB Dart	Monster 13 Sneak	Strong Right 32 Dive
Black	Gun Right 16 Arrow	Strong Right 18 Sweep	Strong Left 33 Dive
Gray	Gun Left 17 Arrow	Tight Slots Jet Sweep	Strong Right Smash
Brown	Gun Right QB Draw	Tight Slots Jet Fake	Steam Right 24 Stretch
Pink	Gun Left QB Draw	Tight Slots 16 BOB	Steam Left Smash
	"SWITCH!" - Stand up, change play		

Example of a play call wristband

to remember their assignments on certain plays. Ideally each of your players can use the same wristband containing just play names. While there is merit to listing position-specific assignments, in youth football players switch positions so often that this carries a high chance for error.

We will discuss gameday operation of the no-huddle in a later chapter. For installation and practice purposes, plan on introducing and using your communication system from the first day. In our case, a thunderstorm came through two-thirds of the way through our first practice, forcing us into our elementary school gym. In that controlled environment we handed out wristbands to each player, explained the language we would be using, then quizzed them with a variety of play calls. After more than half the team answered correctly we were satisfied enough to go forward. On day two, we split our players into two offenses to run plays on air and used the wristbands to signal the plays we wanted to run. They were nearly flawless. To be sure, there will be kids who do not grasp this right away, or even after a few practices. But if the majority of your kids are getting it, forge ahead and work with the stragglers individually to get them up to speed.

Bottom line: If you are hesitant to implement a no-huddle system because you do not think your kids can handle it, think again. Most kids have the smarts to pick it up, and enjoy the challenging of learning a new secret language.

If you are hesitant to implement a no-huddle system because you think it compromises your ability to teach kids football fundamentals, think again. You just need to adapt your coaching style. The massive amount of extra reps your kids get will be worth it.

If you do huddle — hey, no hard feelings! No-huddle is not for everyone. I enjoy watching a well-organized team break the huddle and jog to the line with precision. My preferred play communication here would be to equip your quarterback with a wristband carrying your plays. You do not need to make it as complicated as with a total no-huddle system, but you will need to be somewhat discreet about conveying plays to your quarterback.

Make no mistake about it: creating, installing, practicing, calling, and executing a successful youth football offense can be challenging. But with attention to detail, planning, and repetition you can produce a unit that generates yards and puts points on the board.

Installation

Two important considerations have driven our tactics regarding offensive installation.

1. We have chosen not to distribute a playbook to our kids, either in print or digital format. If a player or their parent asks for it to study on their own we will certainly consider it. But in general, youth football players do not need additional homework. Let them be kids!

2. We do not have access to a classroom setting during practice. In case of severe weather we can take shelter in our elementary school's gymnasium, but by and large all of our activities take place outside.

We begin installing our offense on the first day of practice. A key piece of equipment in this process is a 24- by 36-inch white board. Since purchasing it a couple years ago, we have used this board almost every day to help illustrate formations and assignments for both offense and defense. Chance are you have seen something like this by football coaches diagramming plays — it's not a new concept. But without a classroom we have had to be creative.

For white board sessions we typically gather our players around a goal post on our practice field; our kids have taken to affectionately (if not creatively) calling these periods "Around the Goalpost." One coach holds the white board about waist high, while the coach leading the session manipulates the board from a crouched or kneeling stance. Rather than re-drawing all 22 players each time, we use small circular magnets labeled by position, then use a dark-colored marker to indicate their actions on each play. We never install a new play or make an adjustment to an existing play without first illustrating it on the white board. When teaching and illustrating a new play, be as thorough as possible, explaining every player's assignment, footwork, fakes, and other techniques in maximum detail. Do not expect that kids will just "get it" inherently. The little things matter, and you need to teach them.

On the first day of practice we start with basics like formation names, position names and numbers, hole numbers, etc. We continue this for the first couple days until every player appears to have this information down pat. Test your kids by asking them to identify these elements and recall the plays they have already learned. Do not call only on the kids who clearly know their stuff and always raise their hand. Be sure to engage your newer, weaker, or more introverted players to be sure they understand.

As you illustrate plays, ask your players to articulate why plays are blocked a certain way, or what different motions or fakes are meant to accomplish. You will be surprised by how well they understand play concepts and design. Having kids explain things can in many cases be more effective in helping their peers learn than if the information comes only from you. If you have the time to do it and feel comfortable they will treat the time properly, give the marker to your players and ask them to draw up a play and explain why it will work. You might be pleasantly surprised with what they come up with!

Over the course of the first two weeks of practice, leading up to a scrimmage, we aim to install 2-4 plays per day for the first five or six days. If the calendar works out in such a way that you hold eight practices before scrimmaging, leave at least two days without installing anything new and devote that time to reviewing and repping what you have learned. This will give you enough plays to run in the scrimmage but still leave more to install leading up to the first game or two.

Start by installing your bread and butter plays, and build off them with plays involving similar actions. For instance, 26 Lead can be followed by 26 Bootleg and 26 Bootleg Pass. Similarly, group 3-4 passing plays together to simplify things for your line.

After drawing up plays on the white board, walk through them with an 11-player unit on air. If you have enough players at your disposal, break into two units so each kid gets maximum reps. After this, break into offensive indys before returning to run through plays 11-on-11. This is known as the whole-part-whole method that has gained popularity in teaching and coaching circles. We do not follow this strict progression every practice — as the season progresses it ends up being part-whole more often than not — but showing kids the big picture objective, breaking it into and practicing their individual assignments, then reassembling to practice plays as a unit has proven to be an effective strategy.

Play Names

The plays in this book follow standard naming conventions. In all cases these elements can be altered to suit your preferences. Let's take a look at the play call Strong Right 26 Lead. The basic elements include:

Formation: Instructs offensive players where to line up. For instance, in this book Strong Right calls for the Thunderback to line up to the right side of the formation; the offense has more players to the right side of the center, hence "strong right."

Back number: The first of the two-digit number, in this play 2, indicates which player will carry the ball. For purposes of this book, 1=quarterback, 2=halfback, 3=fullback, 4=Thunderback (or wingback), 5=split end, 6=tight end. In this play the halfback will carry the ball.

Hole number: The second of the two-digit number, in this play 6, indicates which hole the ball carrier will run through. Hole numbers to the right of center are even numbers starting at 2, while hole numbers to the left of center are odd numbers starting at 3. In this play the halfback will run through the 6 hole, which is the hole between the right tackle and tight end.

Action: The last part of the play name indicates any key actions. In this play "lead" indicates that the fullback will lead the halfback through the 6 hole, and the halfback will cut off the fullback's lead block. These actions can be as long and descriptive as you think appropriate, but we suggest keeping play names as short and simple as possible. You are not dealing with NFL players here!

Strong Right 26 Lead

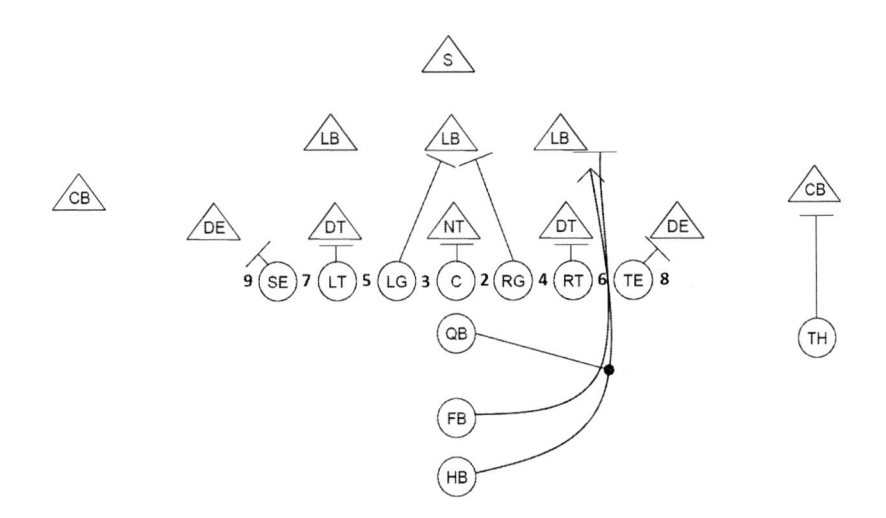

Example of a typical play name

PART 5

Defense and Special Teams

OK, enough offense. Time to talk defense. Time to talk zone blitzes and line stunts and three techniques and cover-two.

Wrong.

As with offense, there is no shortage of concepts for football defenses, and no shortage of experts willing to share their knowledge of these concepts. But for youth football there are really only two words that matter.

Gap responsible.

We will go into this more in depth throughout this chapter, but the idea is simple: if you structure your defense, through alignment, movement, and technique, to account for eight gaps on every single play, chance are you will field an effective defense. Simple, but remember that a good offense will account for all of your defenders and do everything in its power to create just one open hole for a ball carrier to squirt through for positive yardage.

Before going forward, remember that my opinions on defense are influenced by the rules in which our teams compete. Specific to defense:

- Linebackers and cornerbacks may not line up closer than 3 yards to the line of scrimmage, except when the opposing team possesses the ball inside the defensive team's 10-yard-line.
- No more than three linebackers are allowed to line up inside the box — the area between the offensive tackles' outside shoulders.
- No blitzing is allowed.
- Defensive tackles and nose tackles may only align head up on the offensive linemen across from them.
- The standard alignment is a 5-3.

Let's start by talking about what type of player you should be looking for at each position, based on their typical responsibilities.

Positioning Your Players

As with offense, youth football players should get experience playing a variety of defensive positions. Kids' physical attributes will obviously influence this — you are not going to play your heaviest kid at cornerback — but most kids can add value to your defense at multiple spots. Here is what we look for at each position.

Defensive end: In my opinion this is the most important position on a youth football defense. This is because most big plays at this age are outside runs

— give the ball to the fastest kid and let him outrun everyone to the corner. If you can not stop this play, none of the rest of this chapter matters, so pay extra attention to this spot.

The casual football fan hears "defensive end" and thinks Reggie White, Bruce Smith, J.J. Watt. Physically imposing, dominant pass rushers who are also pretty good against the run. If you have a couple kids like this — who are not positionally-restricted by your league's weight rules — then by all means consider playing them at defensive end. In all likelihood, your defensive ends will bear more resemblance physically to outside linebackers in a commonly-seen 3-4 defenses: medium-sized players who are among your best athletes.

Your defensive ends need to be quick off the ball, flexible enough to change directions laterally, strong enough to take on blockers at the point of attack, and disciplined enough to stay at home. All these traits matter, but the last is perhaps the most important. If you have an aggressive, undisciplined end who crashes down the line in pursuit of tackles for loss, he might create several negative-yardage plays but follow that by running himself out of position and giving up a massive running lane on a counter or reverse. While you may put two of your best athletes at defensive end, they may not end up making many tackles. You — and the kids playing this crucial spot — need to have enough trust in their nine teammates to get the job done that you are willing to make this important sacrifice.

Defensive tackle: There is a good chance that who you play at defensive tackle will be influenced by your roster makeup and league weight restrictions. In our league, for example, weight restricted players can play only center, offensive tackle, or defensive tackle. This means that tackles on both sides of the ball usually end up being the biggest kids on the field. This is much like football at older levels, where defensive tackles are typically sturdy and strong. Absent that prototype, it is possible for a quick medium-sized player to excel at this position.

Nose tackle: Medium-sized and quick applies to this position as well. As stated in the previous paragraph, weight restricted players in our conference may not play nose tackle, which eliminates the enormous "war daddy" style of nose seen in the college and NFL ranks. At the other end of the spectrum, over the years we have seen smaller defensive back-sized players take snaps at nose tackle, to varying degrees of effectiveness. Quickness off the snap can be disruptive, but a good center can swallow up a little nose.

Linebacker: The assumption is most youth football teams place their best athletes at linebacker, and in many cases that holds true. My assertion is that while you should definitely not put weaker or minimally experienced players at linebackers, your defense may be better overall with your top players at defensive end or tackle. Above all else, your linebackers need to be disciplined enough to fill gaps, fearless enough to take on and defeat blockers, and — this can not be stressed enough — your best tacklers. In the case of your outside linebackers, they will also need to move laterally and backpedal in performing occasional pass coverage duties.

Cornerback: Typically these are smaller, younger players, although if you are blessed with the right roster makeup you can deploy studs at this position that operate almost as secondary defensive ends. While cornerbacks' assignment is always to play the pass first, they must be able to support the run, defeat stalk blocks, and tackle in space.

Safety: This position has been hotly debated more than any other among the guys I have coached with. Good naturedly of course! We have seen all types play safety, from the most limited, least experienced player on a team to the squad's top athlete. It comes down to your roster composition and philosophy. Can you place a weaker player at safety and put him in position to succeed with 10 stronger ones in front of him? Or would you rather put a stud at safety and have him make plays all over the field and limit big plays by the offense? There is no perfect answer, but how you plan to deploy your safety will influence what type of player you put in that position.

Mind the Gaps

Earlier we asserted that only two words matter in youth football defense: gap responsible. In the event this is a new concept to you, here is a primer.

Much like offensive play directions are labeled by numbered holes between blockers, defenses identify holes as lettered gaps. Unlike the standard with holes, gaps are not separated by an odd-even distinction. The letters are the same moving right and left.

- A gap is the opening between the center and each guard.
- B gap is the opening between guards and tackles.
- C gap is the opening between tackles and tight ends.
- D gap is the space outside the ends.

A gap responsible defense will place a defender in each gap on every play. How a team accomplishes this depends on personnel or an opponent's tendencies. These assignments need not be set in stone and can be changed up to prevent the offense from getting too comfortable with what they are seeing. Earlier I mentioned that a typical defensive alignment in our league is five defensive linemen and three linebackers. Standard gap responsibilities for a 5-3 would be:

Nose tackle: Defense's left A gap. Most centers snap right-handed, which

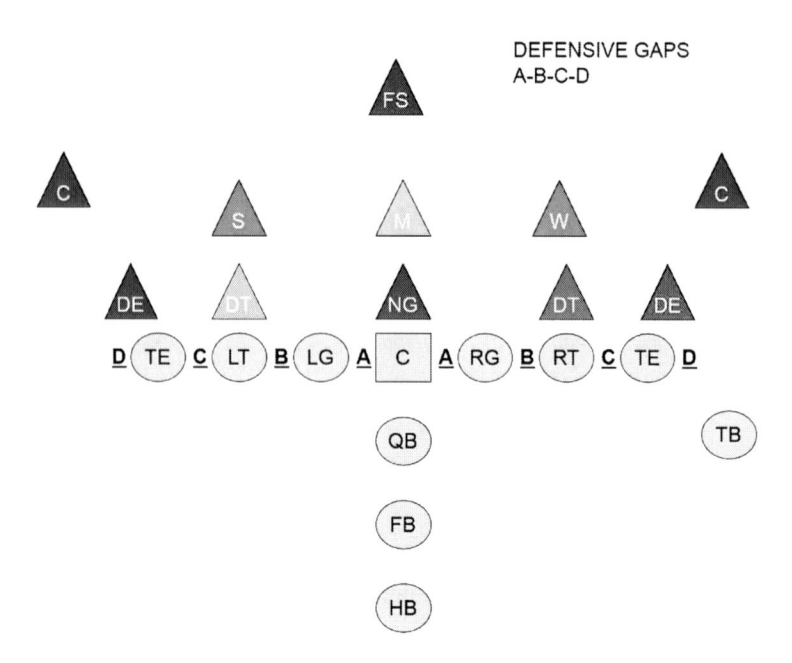

```
                              ▲                DEFENSIVE GAPS
                              FS               A-B-C-D

        ▲          ▲          ▲          ▲              ▲
        C          S          M          W              C

        ▲     ▲         ▲           ▲     ▲
        DE    DT        NG          DT    DE
        D(TE)C(LT)B(LG)A( C )A(RG)B(RT)C(TE)D

                         (QB)              (TB)

                         (FB)

                         (HB)
```

makes it more difficult for them to get a hand up to block movement to his right. Many teams will account for this by giving the center double team help in the form of the right guard.

Middle linebacker: Right A gap.

Outside linebackers: B gaps. Linebackers' jobs are pretty straightforward but often done poorly. There are a variety of ways to teach linebackers to fill and fit gaps, but the bottom line is they need to attack the line of scrimmage post-snap. A common mistake made by kids playing this position is to stand stationary or even retreat a step or two after the snap. This leaves gaps unfilled, and ball carriers exploiting those gaps are met by linebackers who are not in optimal position to make a tackle.

Defensive tackles: C gaps. Linebacker-tackle gap responsibilities are often interchangeable and driven by personnel. Sending tackles to the C gaps focuses a bit more beef on pushing runs back inside.

Defensive ends: D gaps. Those D gaps are enormous compared to the others, which is why your defensive ends are so important.

Cornerbacks and safety: Defensive backs' assignment is typically to play the pass first, support the run second. Cornerbacks will serve as backup to the defensive ends. Safeties can act as erasers for any number of breakdowns that happen in the front eight. We have also seen safeties play closer to the line in a role almost like that of a linebacker, although our league rules stipulate no more than three linebackers can align in the box.

In past football viewing or reading, you may have come across the terms "one gap" or "two gap" defensive linemen. As the names imply, a one gap lineman is responsible for a single gap in the opposing offensive blocking, whereas a two gap lineman is responsible for the gap on either side of the offensive lineman in front of him. While both approaches are used at higher levels of football and both have merit, most kids playing defensive line in youth football are neither strong nor mentally experienced enough to read and react to plays in the manner asked of two gap linemen.

There is more than one way to fill gaps. Any youth football defense needs to be built off this simple but absolutely critical premise.

Pass Defense

Against a typical opponent, a youth football defense will be defending the run 80-90 percent of the time. Those 8-10 passes they are facing are not exactly being thrown by Joe Montana to Jerry Rice. Still, most youth quarterbacks will be able to complete a pass to a receiver who has no one within 10 yards of him, so you can not forget about pass defense altogether.

Start with your cornerbacks. These two should always be in a pass-first mindset, and as the defenders lined up across from the offense's split receivers will be responsible for covering those players first. Then decide how you would prefer to cover tight ends releasing into pass patterns. An outside linebacker makes sense, as does a safety. Part of this will be determined whether you play man-to-man or zone coverage. Man is the easier concept for kids to grasp, but with the right players zone can be effective as well.

At some point you will be confronted with unbalanced receiver sets like twins (two receivers split to one side), trips (three receivers), quads (four receivers), or double twins (two receivers split to each side). While much of how you respond is influenced by the rest of the offense's alignment and their tendencies, simple defensive alignment adjustments include bumping a defensive end or linebacker outside, or moving over a safety. Be wary of overcommitting bodies to these formations that seem to indicate pass: many times offenses align this way to create a more advantageous defensive box to run against.

In terms of pass rush, earlier we mentioned luminary defensive end names like White, Smith, and Watt. If you have big, dominant pass rushers like these guys, they will likely be playing inside at defensive tackle rather than defensive end. Similar to their role in run defense, your ends need to be able to set the edge and guard against a quarterback scrambling to evade the interior pass rush. Instructing your ends to pin their ears back and attack the passer is a risky strategy, leaving you vulnerable to big runs. Plan on your pass rush coming from your interior three linemen and middle linebacker.

Firebirds Scouting Report
Team
Date
Coach

○○●○○

○○●○○

○○●○○

Sample scout sheet

Scouting

You may have read this subhead and winced. Scouting in youth football? Isn't that a bit much? While I can certainly understand people who take that position, my personal view is that it is worth the investment.

You are teaching your players the game of football. During the course of installing and practicing your offense, defense, and special teams, they will learn one way of doing things and why a football team would do them. Maybe you run a Wing-T offense, and on defense instruct your tackles to crash the B gap. Gathering information on your opponents' personnel and schemes offers you the opportunity to teach other approaches to the game, broadening their experience.

You can never learn enough about the game and how it is played at your level. Even the most successful veteran coaches are constantly evaluating the way other teams operate in a search for ways to improve. The fact you are reading this book suggests you are interested in personal growth and development. Scouting will move you along in your growth and development as a youth football coach.

The more you know about your opponents, and are able to prepare your kids for what they will encounter during games, the more likely they are to experience success. If they experience success, they are more likely to have fun. If they have fun, they are more likely to continue playing football as they get older. The sample scout sheet on page 99 is a template you can use to draw up other teams' plays. Five linemen are static, you draw the other six players and their actions.

Ultimately scouting is not absolutely necessary. You can prepare your team for a variety of offensive and defensive concepts generically and they will be just fine. And to be clear, we are not suggesting putting your kids through extensive film sessions. They will have plenty of time for that in high school. But if you have the time and desire, taking a look at what teams around your league are doing is worth the investment.

Special Teams

Since this is a chapter about defense, we will first address the two special teams that involve tackling the opponent: kickoff and punt team. Your objective with these two units is simple: do not let the other team score on a return. Picking up field position, winning the "hidden yardage" battle — those are nice goals and if you can do those within the context of preventing the other team from scoring, good on you. But that should be your secondary goal.

Why so paranoid? Think about it: if you attempt a traditional deep kickoff or punt, chances are that kick is being fielded by the other team's fastest, most elusive runner. He is taking possession in a wide open space with all sorts of running options. Your tacklers, even if they are among your best, are running full speed. All sorts of bad things can happen! Here is how I suggest you approach these units.

Punt: Don't. I'm serious! Even putting the very real considerations of the last paragraph aside, ask yourself how many yards of field position you can gain by punting. This is not the NFL, and you do not have a punter who can boom it

50 yards with 5 seconds of hang time. In all likelihood, your absolute best case scenario is a punt that travels 25-30 yards in the air, and a net gain of about 20 yards. That is certainly not worth sacrificing one more attempt at a first down, let alone the risk of conceding a touchdown. Will there be times when you absolutely can not avoid punting? Sure — when you are backed up inside your own 10-yard-line facing fourth-and-20-plus yards, or something approaching that doomsday scenario. With your back up against that wall, instruct your punter to angle the kick sharply toward your sideline and put your best tacklers on that side. If the punt sails out of bounds, so be it — the other team did not score.

From a play calling perspective, beginning a series with the knowledge that you have four plays to generate 10 yards, rather than the traditional three, gives you much more flexibility. Rather than needing to average 3.3 yards per play, you only need to average 2.5. You can get away with being 25 percent less efficient on a down-to-down basis by not artificially limiting the number of plays you will run. Alternatively, you have an additional opportunity to spring an explosive play of 20-plus yards, which is always a key contributor to offensive success.

Kickoff: This kick requires more nuanced thinking than a punt, because unlike a punt, many kids are able to blast kicks off a tee a substantial distance. It is not unusual to see a youth football kicker (starting from his own 40-yard-line) boot a kickoff to the receiving team's 30- or 25-yard-line. If you can cover that effectively using traditional kickoff coverage tactics — some form of your coverage players staying in their lanes — you can really set the opposing offense back at a disadvantageous starting spot.

My suggestion, however, is that you onside kick. Every time. At least until you are up by a running clock score and continuing to onside kick would be unsportsmanlike. The basic rationale is the same as articulated earlier: onside kicks are less likely to be returned for touchdowns, or even long gains, than deep kickoffs. The most likely scenario is the other team recovers the kick for no or minimal return. The worst-case scenario is the kick bounces out of bounds and you are penalized. In the best-case scenario, you recover the kick and go back on offense.

There are all sorts of onside kicks. Whatever type you use, though, angle it toward the sideline. This limits the options an opposing returner has if he fields the ball cleanly. It also funnels possible returns toward the three or four strong tacklers you put on that side. After a while, other teams will catch on to this strategy. They may send out a hands team to return your kicks. If they have scouted your team, they may work on this in practice. While this might decrease the element of surprise and the optimal effectiveness of your onside kicks, at the very least you are taking your opponent out of its comfort zone. And most importantly, not letting them score on the return!

For a fascinating read on a coach who employs these tactics at a higher level, look up coach Kevin Kelley of Pulaski Academy in Arkansas. Kelley has been called "unconventional" and "rogue" for avoiding punts and traditional kickoffs, but his approach is backed by thorough statistical analysis. Kelley's willingness to win radically outweighs his fear of losing traditionally.

Punt return: Hopefully your defense will be strong enough to force opposing offense into plenty of fourth down situations. If you do, chances are even if your opponents are not totally in the "never punt" camp, for the reasons articulated earlier you will see far fewer punts than would be seen in a typical college or NFL game. Do not spend much practice time on punt return. In our league, offenses need to declare whether or not they will be punting on fourth down, and can not fake a punt. Without the need to guard against a fake, send your shiftiest two or three players deep to field the punt, and instruct the other eight or nine kids to block the guys in front of them. A simple approach, sure, and there are certainly more sophisticated ways to approach this phase of the game. But consider how much practice time you want to devote to a play that might happen once or twice per game.

Kickoff return: When planning for this phase it helps to know something about your opponent. If they favor onside or pooch kicks, you will need to use more skilled kids in your front line or two. If they typically kick deep, you can get away with using less experienced players up front. Either way, you can never stress enough that these kicks are live balls that need to be recovered once they go 10 yards. For a standard alignment, we use five players in front, 10 yards from the kicker; four players in the second line, positioned in the gaps between the front five, 7 or 8 yards behind the front line; and two players deep, depth depending on the opposing kicker's leg strength.

Placekicking: In the hundreds of youth football games I have seen over the years, only one has featured a made field goal. However, many have featured successful point after touchdown kicks, which in our league are especially valuable: PAT kicks count for two points, as opposed to one point for a PAT scored by run or pass. As with other special teams, do not devote huge amounts of time to placekicking. But it pays to find out early if you have one or two kids capable of making what amounts to a 15- or 20-yard kick.

At some point during your first three weeks of practice, give every player a chance or two at an extra point-length kick. If you are using a standard placekicking block, consider having a coach serve as holder; for this introductory exercise you can also use a kickoff tee, moving to a block once you have identified the finalists. It will not take long for the group of potential kickers to narrow your team into a handful of kids who can reasonably be expected to convert a kick in a game. Urge them to work on this skill before or after practice, devoting only a handful of full-team reps (complete with snap) to this activity during the week.

The give-everyone-a-shot approach works well for punting and kickoffs. It is worth doing this even if you have a strong idea of who you want performing these duties. Sometimes a new kid or a returnee who has matured will surprise you. With punts and kickoffs, you can break your kids into groups of four or five and give them each two or three shots, then take the winners of each group hold a final competition. This shows your players that the job is merit-based, and does not take as long as you would think. These kicking competitions are a good change of pace from the grind of preseason practice.

PART 6

Game Day

You have planned and run efficient practices. Installed a logical offense and sound defense. It's game day!

This is why you and your kids put in all that hard work. Everyone looks great in their uniforms. The national anthem plays. Players are introduced by the public address announcer. They run through a banner. Grandma and Grandpa cheer from the stands. It's as American as apple pie.

If you are human, you will have butterflies in your stomach, same as your kids. But if you have prepared properly during the days, weeks, and months leading up to game day, this should be the easy part of the football coaching experience.

Practice Preparation

You may think that every single practice activity you run with your team is preparation for game day, and you are correct. Blocking, tackling, running plays on offense, lining up correctly on defense — all of that is part of the game. What I mean here, though, is devoting practice time specifically to functions that happen only on game day. Consider practicing these things during the week, or at very least in the week leading up to your first game.

Getting there: Specify when you want your players to arrive at the field; one hour before game time is plenty of time. If you are playing a road game, give your players an estimated travel time to the venue from your home community. This information should be repeated several times throughout the course of the week with your players and with their families via your preferred communication methods. Included in this communication should be reminders that kids get a good night of sleep prior to the game, eat a light breakfast, and bring every single piece of equipment to the game.

It never fails to amaze me how many kids forget to bring a jersey or some other critical piece of equipment, which often results in them missing a half of action. A good tip shared by one of our veteran coaches is to provide players with a checklist and instruct them to physically touch each item before they leave the house.

Warmups: Game day warmups will be similar to your practice warmups, but perhaps in a compressed time. Also, consider that on game day you may not have access to a perfectly lined field with marked 5-yard increments. In addition to your dynamic warmups and any stretching, practice running some offensive plays, lining up correctly on defense, and reviewing special teams personnel. Warmups, at least in our league, end with our players lining up numerically and heading to the designated spot for pregame weigh-in.

Introductions: You may not know exactly how your team will be introduced at a road game, but chances are it will be similar to how you do it on your home turf. Similarly, instruct your team how you would like them to line up for the national anthem. If you have the time, actually doing these things can be a short, fun way to break the monotony of preseason practice, and will go a long way toward making your team look sharp and feel prepared on game day.

Chant: It may seem silly, but a well-executed huddle chant can set the right tone for your team before a game. Conversely, a weak, disjointed chant can set a tone of doubt. Involve your kids in determining your team's pregame chant, and how you will break a whole-team huddle, but keep it simple.

Coin toss: Select your captains during the week and practice the coin toss with them. Your kids need to know exactly what you want to do whether you win or lose the toss. Most officials are great about working with kids and helping them avoid embarrassing mistakes, but do not overlook this important detail.

Substitution: On air, practice running offensive plays while moving up and down the field. Have a coach spot the ball after each play, using realistic placement in relation to the hash marks. Call a penalty on your team every once in a while — it will happen on game day. While this is happening, your players not in the game should practice where to stand on the sideline in relation to the play caller and coach managing substitutions. Practice making those substitutions. Simulate scores, changes of possessions, special teams — anything that may occur in the game.

Play calling: Your offensive coordinator should practice calling plays using the communication system you will be using on game day. Ideally you will have been using this system during team offense sessions throughout the week. But in a game preparation setting, be sure to take the play clock into consideration. You don't have all day to get your play in!

Stoppages: Establish a protocol for how your team will act during stoppages of play like timeouts, quarter breaks, or halftime. Cover details like how players will get water, when coaches and players will speak, etc. In the heat of the battle this may go out the window, but establishing a plan gives you a shot at making optimal use of breaks in play.

This list is a good start but certainly not exhaustive. Let your mind run free and think about all of the possible scenarios that might arise on game day, and address them with your team ahead of time. There is no better cure for game day nerves than preparation and the knowledge that you and your team have done everything possible to get ready.

Coaching Responsibilities

Just as with practice, maximize all of your available coaching resources. A youth football game has so many moving parts that one person can be overwhelmed if tasked with handling all of them. Here is a suggested method for distributing game day responsibilities among your coaching staff.

Warmups: Ideally a coach other than the head coach or coordinators will supervise warmups/dynamic stretching. After that piece is completed, the offensive coordinator oversees the run-through of plays likely to be called during the game. If enough players and coaches are available, and if time and space permit, consider running two offensive units on air to maximize reps. Next, the defensive coordinator reviews considerations for that side of the ball, followed by special teams lineups.

Weigh-in: If your league has weight restrictions for certain positions, you will likely be required to weigh your players before the game. Designate one coach to oversee this process before every game. He will be responsible for monitoring not just your team's weights but also your opponent's. If you or the team you are facing has a player whose weight borders on restricted or unrestricted, your coach should pay special attention to their weight and report to you on any change in status. Instruct your players that if they need to use the restroom, do it immediately after weigh-in.

Meet with officials: As head coach, make a point to introduce yourself to the officiating crew before the game. This might be difficult if you do not play the first game of the day, but there should still be time to touch base before kickoff. Let them know your name and the fact that you appreciate their contributions to youth football. Ask if they have any questions regarding your league's rules and clarify if they do. Notify them of any trick or otherwise non-standard plays you plan to run, to lessen the risk of them making the wrong call based on an assumption. Consider introducing them to your captains responsible for receiving on-field communication. If you are hosting, offer them a drink or snack from the concession stand, and be sure they are paid the agreed-upon rate.

It should go without saying, but making friendly banter with the referees is not just a pregame activity. Treat officials with respect. They have a difficult job and are doing their best. It is possible to express disagreement or disappointment with officiating decisions in a firm manner without acting like a lunatic. Ranting and raving at officials not only makes you look foolish, but it

SUBSTITUTION PLAN
8-24-18 vs. West Town

LCB	LDE	LS	LDT	LLB	NT	RLB	RDT	RS	RDE	RCB		Positions	
Aiden	Logan	Daniel	Thulien	Lucas	Jacob	Ethan	Joseph	Elijah	Alex	Mason		Henry	LG, RG, NT
Michael	Jacob	Jacob	Jackson	Daniel	Sam	Elijah	Brian	Ethan	Jacob	Ben		Oliver	LG, RG, CB
Liam				Matthew	Henry		William			Oliver		Matthew	RG, LG, CB, LB
												Liam	RG, LG, CB, LB
												William	LT, DT
Q	**H**	**F**	**Y**	**Z**	**X**	**LT**	**LG**	**C**	**RG**	**RT**		Jackson	LG, RG, LT, DT
Daniel	Ethan	Jacob	Elijah	Logan	Mason	Thulien	Jackson	Sam	Aiden	Joseph		Aiden	CB, RG, LG, LB

Starting in Packer (above): When done with that, switch to normal first team, with Ben replacing Mason

Daniel	Logan	Ethan	Elijah	Jacob	Ben	Thulien	Jackson	Brian	Aiden	Joseph		Sam	C, DT, LT
												Ben	X, C, CB

After 7 plays: William to LT, Jacob out, Thulien to Z; Henry to LG, Jackson out; Matthew to RG, Aiden out
After a couple plays off Jacob subs in for whoever needs break; Mason some at X or Y, Alex at X or F, Lucas at Y

Daniel	Logan	Ethan	Elijah	Thulien	Ben	William	Henry	Brian	Matthew	Joseph		Joseph	RT, DT, LT
												Thulien	LT, DT, Z, NT
												Alex	DE, F, X, Z

After 14 plays: Oliver to LG, Henry out; Aiden or Liam to RG, Matthew out; Jacob back to Z, Thulien to LT, William out
Lucas/Mason/Alex rotate in to give Daniel, Ethan, Logan, Elijah breaks

Daniel	Logan	Ethan	Elijah	Jacob	Mason	Thulien	Oliver	Brian	Aiden	Joseph		Michael	CB, H, Y
												Mason	CB, Y, X
												Lucas	LS, Q, Y, CB, LB
												Logan	H, DE, Y
												Elijah	Y, RS, CB, LB, H, Q
												Jacob	Z, NT, F, DT, H, Q

Offense Depth Chart

Q	H	F	Y	Z	X	LT	LG	C	RG	RT
Daniel	Logan	Ethan	Elijah	Jacob	Ben	Thulien	Jackson	Brian	Aiden	Joseph
Lucas	Michael	Alex	Lucas	Thulien	Mason	William	Henry	Ben	Liam	Thulien
Jacob	Elijah	Jacob	Mason	Logan	Alex	Alex	Oliver	Matthew	Matthew	Aiden
	Ethan									

Anywhere: Daniel, Jacob, Alex, Ethan, Thulien   RT-LT: Jackson

Ethan — F, LB, H, DT, Q
Daniel — Q, LB, F, H, LS

Kickoff Team

	1	2	3	4	5	6	7	8	9	10	11
Our Sideline	Mason	Elijah	Alex	Matthew	Aiden	Liam Yelier	Lucas kicker	Ben	Oliver	Jackson	Henry

Kick Return

Liam		Oliver		Ben		Jackson		Henry
	Alex		Matthew		Aiden		Lucas	
		Mason			Elijah			

Punt Team
Offense, with Matthew and Oliver replacing Joseph/Jackson/William

Punt Return
First team defense, with Sam replacing Joseph

Example of a substitution plan/depth chart

sets a bad example for your kids.

Substitution: Before every game put in writing a substitution plan to ensure every one of your players receives their fair share of playing time. An example can be seen above, but yours need not be this detailed. A helpful component of this is listing each player along with all of the positions they have repped at during practice, in the event you have to put them in the game in a position outside your original plan.

Anticipate at least one player being late, sick, without key equipment, or a complete no-show. Ideally parents will communicate these things as early as possible, but you need to be ready for anything. Also, more often than not game circumstances will throw a wrench into your plans and you will be forced to play kids at positions that may not be optimal. Plan for as many contingencies as possible and you will be equipped to handle these hiccups more smoothly.

Designate one coach responsible for tracking plays. This coach should communicate players' status with a second coach, possibly the coordinator whose unit is not on the field, or a different coach altogether. That coach then assembles players on the sideline for entry into the game and communication with players coming off the field. Substitutions can be frenetic even in the smoothest of circumstances, but advance planning, organization, and communication can make it less of a nightmare.

Offense: Each week your offensive coordinator should produce a call sheet and distribute copies to every coach who wants one. We are not talking about the comically large, Denny's menu-sized pieces NFL coaches use. If you have that many plays for a youth football team, you're doing it wrong. You should be able to fit everything needed for your offense on an 8-½ by 11-inch sheet of paper. Depending on how much information you want at your disposal — and how good your eyes are — your call sheet could include the following information:

2018 Firebirds

Play Count Sheet

Firebirds vs. _____   Date _____

	1	2	3	4	5	6	7		1	2	3	4	5	6	7
Daniel D/O															
Ethan D/O															
Jacob D/O															
Elijah D/O															
Logan D/O															
Lucas D/O															
Mason D/O															
Michael D/o/KR															
Alex D/o/KO/KR															
Joseph d/O/KO/KR															
Ben d/o/KO/KR															
Sam D/o/KR															
Aiden d/O/KO/KR															
Jackson d/O/KO															
William D/O/KO/KR															
Liam d/o/KO/KR															
Matthew d/o/KO/KR															
Oliver d/o/KO/KR															
Ryan d/o/KO/KR															

Example of a play count sheet

1. A list of all your plays. These could be grouped by runs/passes, right/left, down/distance, etc. If you use the wristband color/number communication system described earlier, consider listing three or four possible combinations for each play, so you are not constantly consulting a wristband to come up with something from scratch.

2. A script of your first 10 or 15 plays. The concept and rationale of scripting plays is well documented. In reality, game circumstances will often throw you off script within a few plays. But creating a script is still a worthwhile exercise for conceptualizing the order in which you would like to call plays, especially complementary ones. Scripting also creates a logical order for running plays during practice and pregame.

3. Offense notes. For instance, last season we committed to passing more. In

Firebird play call sheet	8-24-18 vs. West Town	Depth	
RUNS RIGHT		Q	Daniel
Strong Right 26 Stretch: Black 761, Black 319, Black 165			Ethan
Strong Right 28 Pitch: White 291, White 169, White 713			Lucas
Strong Right 18 Sprint: Yellow 771, Yellow 318, Yellow 144		H	Elijah
Monster Right 24 Stretch: Purple 721, Purple 814, Purple 126			Alex
Pro Right 34 Counter: Orange 872, Orange 149, Orange 245			Ethan
Pro Right 38 Pitch: White 832, White 324, White 269		F	Jacob
Tight Slots Jet Fake: Pink 762, Pink 329, Pink 275			Ethan
Strong Right 32 Dive: Green 573, Green 739, Green 326			Aiden
Monster Right 13 Sneak: Purple 823, Purple 472, Purple 312		Y	Mason
			Oliver
			Lucas
RUNS LEFT		X	Liam
Strong Left 27 Stretch: Orange 121, Orange 914, Orange 148			Noah
Strong Left 29 Pitch: Blue 561, Blue 819, Blue 415			James
Strong Left 19 Sprint: Yellow 872, Yellow 728, Yellow 243		Z	Ben
Tight Jet Pitch: Purple 662, Purple 828, Purple 423			Noah
Strong Left 33 Dive: Orange 123, Orange 534, Orange 916			Liam
		LT	Sam
			Joseph
PASSES RIGHT			Henry
Strong Right Z Corner: Gray 782, Gray 216, Gray 587		LG	Matthew
Strong Right Y Go Z Out: Red 292, Red 625, Red 362			Aiden
Strong Right 27 Bootleg: Gray 521, Gray 817, Gray 229			Henry
Monster Right Play Action: Pink 741, Pink 349, Pink 187		C	Jackson
Slots Two Go: Blue 767, Blue 333, Blue 923			Sam
			Aiden
PASSES LEFT		RG	Aiden
Strong Left Z Corner: Gray 123, Gray 734, Gray 197			Henry
Strong Left Y Go Z Out: Red 933, Red 643, Red 617			Matthew
Slots Quick Hit: White 793, White 732, White 946		RT	Lucas
Strong Left 26 Bootleg: Red 222, Red 818, Red 391			Matthew
			Liam

Offense notes
Stay Aggressive
Throw
Run Packer

Opponent defense
Aggressive ends

FIRST 20 - Packer then ...
1. Gun Right/Left Z Corner
2. Gun Right/Left 26/27 Stretch
3. Gun Right/Left 32/33 Dive
4. Gun Right/Left Y Go Z Out
5. Tight Slots Jet Sweep
6. Strong Left 19 Pitch Sprint
7. Strong Right 32 Fake
8. Slots Quick
9. Strong Pro Right 34 Counter
10. Strong Right/Left 26/27 Stretch
11. Slots Two Go
12. Gun Right/Left 18/19 Sprint
13. Gun Pro Right 38 Pitch
14. Tight Slots 47 Jet Fake
15. Strong Right/Left 26/27 Stretch
16. Strong Left Pro 39 Pitch
17. Monster Right 24 Stretch
18. Strong Right/Left Z Corner
19. Strong Right/Left 32/33 Dive
20. Machine Gun Left 19 Sprint

Example of an offensive play sheet

addition to asking several coaches to remind me to call passing plays if we were getting run-heavy, I made notes on my call sheet with that reminder.

4. Defense notes. If your scouting has revealed opposing players to avoid or

a specific area of their defense to target, note them here.

5. An offensive depth chart. You should know your two- or three-deep by heart, but in the heat of battle it does not hurt to have this information written down.

The bulk of the offensive duties fall on the coordinator, who will be calling plays. But that does not mean everyone else relaxes when you have the ball. Ask each coach (other than the play counter) to monitor a specific area during every play. Maybe it is how your guards are blocking the opposing nose tackle and linebackers. Maybe you want more detail on how aggressively the opposing defensive ends are crashing. Maybe you need to know how fast the opposing cornerbacks appear to be. The coordinator can not see everything — use all of your eyes to gather as much intelligence as possible.

Defense: Coordinating a youth football defense on game day is not quite as complicated as running the offense. But it is every bit as important, if not more. The defensive coordinator's chief priority is making sure the unit is properly aligned to defend the offensive formation. He makes any gap responsibility or pass coverage calls and reminds players of their keys. If the opposition has been well scouted, he may offer a reminder of the team's favorite plays to run in certain situations.

As with offense, task other coaches with focusing on specific players or actions that the coordinator might not be able to see while taking the big picture view. Certain plays may need regular reminders, like instructing cornerbacks to play the pass first, or reminding defensive linemen to watch the snap and not jump offside.

Regarding coordinators, it is important that your players do not bother them on the sideline while their unit is on the field with anything other than a matter of great importance, like a serious injury. If a kid has to use the restroom, or is asking to play defensive line, or needs his chin strap buckled, he should know to ask a coach who is not directing the 11 players currently in action.

Injury/equipment coordinator: Maybe "coordinator" is a bit much in describing this coach's role, but it is an important one nonetheless. Over the course of a game you will invariably have kids come out with injuries of varying degrees. If your team is fortunate, these will be minor bumps and bruises that do not knock a player out of a game. Designate a non-play calling coach to tend to kids who get nicked up, either until they are ready to go back in or until an onsite nurse or other medical personnel arrive to assist. Obviously more serious injuries require the head coach's full attention, and play will stop until appropriate medical attention is given to the injured child.

Regarding equipment, a variety of equipment issues can arise during the course of a game, from the aforementioned unbuckled chin strap to shoulder pads coming unfastened, from mouth guards being lost to shoelaces breaking. Designate a coach to be the point person for handling these issues. That person should be deeply familiar with your box of medical supplies and equipment repair/replacement kits.

Ball/tee boy: As inclusion of the word "boy" in these roles implies, these roles do not need to be filled by adults and can instead be performed by one of your players' siblings. Serving in this capacity is a great way to keep a former player from your program involved, or introduce a future player to the sidelines.

Both jobs are important in smooth game operations, and we have had coaches do them in the past. Of the two, ball boy is probably more important. You don't want your offense to be stuck using anything other than your preferred football. Responsibility for tees pertains not only to kickoffs, but also the block used for point after touchdown kicks and the rare field goal attempt. The latter often gets forgotten in an equipment bag on the sideline. If you plan to kick extra points, display it prominently on the bench or equipment table, or have the tee boy carry it with him.

Video

A videographer should be a vital part of your game day operations. Recording video does not necessarily help in real time — our league has rules prohibiting communication devices relaying information to sideline coaching staff — but is a valuable tool in properly teaching your kids in subsequent practices. Video shows things players did well, things they need to work on, and makes sure you do not miss any of it.

Video recording need not be the domain of a member of your coaching staff who works with the team every day. Over the years we have had fathers, mothers, grandparents, and siblings record video, and all have done a good job. There are a variety of ways to record video usable for coaching review. For several years we have used a Canon Vixia camera, originally purchased for several hundred dollars, and a mid-level tripod. Any inexpensive camera could work, including an iPad or iPhone with enough storage.

Our videographers set this equipment up in the press box in one of the

Hudl interface: phone (top) and desktop (middle and bottom)

sections typically reserved for coaching staffs or radio crews. We ask them to record each play individually, starting a second or so before the snap and concluding at the end of the play. Following games, we upload these individual clips to Hudl, the most widely-used service for sports video sharing. In the past year Hudl eliminated the youth team option, leading to a significant increase in our rates. But with its tagging, illustration, mobile friendliness, and sharing capabilities, Hudl is a fantastic option for storing and reviewing video.

In addition to games, consider filming team segments of your practices. The rationale is the same as for recording on game day — to get a more comprehensive, clear-eyed view of what your players need to improve, and also what they are doing well. You do not need a dedicated videographer or elevated perch like you might see at a college practice. Just place a camera on a tripod behind the action, press record, and ask a coach to periodically move the camera forward and backward depending on the action. As with scouting, recording video of practice is definitely more of a luxury than a necessity, but finding time and resources to do it can help you better serve your kids.

Another practice video idea: if you or one of your players' families have a GoPro camera and the proper mount, consider using that in practice setting that would be otherwise unavailable during games. As an example, we have placed a GoPro on our quarterback's helmet during team offense scrimmage sessions, and found out that he was not seeing receivers cleanly. We adjusted his footwork to make certain passing plays designed rollouts. On the other side of the ball, we have placed a GoPro on our middle linebacker's helmet to track his line of sight as plays develop pre- and post-snap. This can be a fun wrinkle to help keep practice from getting stale, and yield some valuable coaching points.

A final note on video: if you are so inclined, use the game video you capture to compile statistics. I started doing this several years ago because:

1. My dad kept stats for our Little League baseball team, and they are fun to look back on 30 years later. Hopefully my boys will feel the same way as adults.

2. One year, the majority of our carries and touchdowns were accumulated by just two of our players. I was looking for a way to quantify all of our kids' contributions and started keeping track of tackles. By the end of the season every player on the team had made the stat sheet, and a variety of players led us in individual categories. That said, we have never shared individual statistics with our players during the season, just team statistics. If you do keep individual stats, use your best judgment on whether your players are mature enough to consume them.

3. There are coaching points to be gleaned from statistics. Taking a look at the cold, hard numbers can reveal if you are running to one side too often, not passing enough, giving too many carries to one kid. Stats can also show which facets of the game contribute most to your team's success, and therefore which activities to emphasize in practice.

4. I am a nerd.

Compiling statistics is fairly time-consuming, but I have found it to be a relaxing Sunday morning activity following games. Every year I get a little more efficient at it, and can now get through a game in about two hours. In order to do this, you need comprehensive video of your games — every play with a wide-angle view that encompasses the yard-line markers along the sideline as well as the down marker. Finally, you need a passing knowledge of, and tolerance for, working with Microsoft Excel or a similar spreadsheet application.

at West Randall
9/18/2018

Game	Play	QTR	Away	AS	Home	HS	Offense	Down	Dist	3con?	4con?	YdLine	Start?	Hash	Formation	Stron	PlayType	Direction	Runner/Int	Yds	TD?	Explosive?	Complete?	Turnover?	Miscue	Special Teams?	Comment
1	33	2	Bloomville	19	WR		0 Bloomville	1	G			2		M	Monster	Y	Run	Middle	Landon	2	Y						
1	34	2	Bloomville	25	WR		0 Bloomville					3		M	Monster	Y	Pass	Right	Will			N (LL)					
1	35	2	Bloomville	25	WR		0																			Bloomville kickoff	
1	36	2	Bloomville	25	WR		0 WR	1	10			56	Y	L			Run	Right		3							
1	37	2	Bloomville	25	WR		0 WR	2	7			53		M			Run	Left		2							
1	38	2	Bloomville	25	WR		0 WR	3	5	N		50		L			Run	Middle		-4						WR fumble	
1	39	2	Bloomville	25	WR		0 Bloomville	1	10			46	Y	R	Strong Left	Y	Pass	Left	Ryan	15				Y (Lebron)			
1	40	2	Bloomville	25	WR		0 Bloomville	1	10			31		R	Strong Right	Y	Run	Right	Michael	1							
1	41	2	Bloomville	25	WR		0 Bloomville	2	9			30		R	Strong Left	Y	Run	Left	David	10							
1	42	2	Bloomville	25	WR		0 Bloomville	1	10			20		M	Strong Right	Y	Run	Middle	Lebron	-3						Bloomville fumble	
1	43	2	Bloomville	25	WR		0 WR	1	10			77	Y	M			Run	Right		-7							
1	44	2	Bloomville	25	WR		0 WR	2	17			84		R			Pass	Right					N				
1	45	2	Bloomville	25	WR		0 WR	3	17	N		84		R			Run	Left		-1							
1	46	2	Bloomville	25	WR		0 WR	4	18		N	85		M			Pass	Left					N				
1	47	2	Bloomville	25	WR		0 WR	1	10			15	Y	M			Pass	Right	Elijah				N (LL)				
1	48	3	Bloomville	25	WR		0																			West Randall kickoff	
1	49	3	Bloomville	25	WR		0 Bloomville	1	10			55	Y	R	Monster	Y	Run	Right	Landon	35	Y						
1	50	3	Bloomville	25	WR		0 Bloomville	1	10			20		M	Monster	Y	Pass	Left	Brian				N (LL)		Interception		
1	51	3	Bloomville	25	WR		0 WR	1	10			88	Y	M			Run	Right		3							
1	52	3	Bloomville	25	WR		0 WR	2	7			85		M			Run	Right		1							
1	53	3	Bloomville	25	WR		0 WR	3	6	Y		84		M			Pass	Left		15		Y					
1	54	3	Bloomville	25	WR		0 WR	1	10			69		M			Run	Right		3							
1	55	3	Bloomville	25	WR		0 WR	2	8			66		R			Pass	Right		0			N				
1	56	3	Bloomville	25	WR		0 WR	3	6	N		70		M			Run	Right		-2							
1	57	3	Bloomville	25	WR		0 WR	4	10		N	70		M			Run	Right		-5							
1	58	3	Bloomville	25	WR		0 Bloomville	1	10			25		M	Strong Right	Y	Run	Right	Lebron	5							
1	59	3	Bloomville	25	WR		0 Bloomville	2	5			20		R	Strong Left	Y	Pass	Left	Elijah	20	Y			Y (Lebron)			
1	60	3	Bloomville	31	WR		0 Bloomville					3		M	Strong Right	Y	Run	Middle	Will	-3							
1	61	3	Bloomville	31	WR		0																			Bloomville kickoff	

Individual Summary

Rushing

Rushing	Rushes	Yards	Yards/Carr	TD	PAT
Mateo	43	397	9.23	9	1
Ryan	45	244	5.42	2	0
Nathan	33	172	5.21	1	1
Isaiah	19	147	7.74	3	1
Thomas	7	23	3.29	1	1
Christian	12	16	1.33	0	0
Eli	2	21	10.50	0	0
Asher	10	2	0.20	0	0
Cameron	2	0	0.00	0	0
Ezra	1	0	0.00	0	0
Dominic	1	0	0	0	0

Receiving

Receiving	Receptions	Yards	Yards/Rec	TD	
Thomas	20	124	6.20	2	0
Cameron	13	121	9.31	2	3
Thulien	8	133	16.63	1	1
Eli	4	51	12.75	0	0

Passing

Passing	Comp	Att	Yards	TD	Int
Mateo	31	59	253	3	1
Asher	8	14	104	2	1
Ryan	5	7	72	1	2

Return Touchdowns

	INT	FR	Punt
Eli	1		
Thomas		1	
Ryan	1		

Rushing (by opponent)

Mateo	Rushes	Yards	Yards/Carr	TD	PAT
West Randall	4	60	15.00	1	0
Anderson	13	57	4.38	3	0
Millersburg	5	59	11.80	1	1
Wonnace	4	69	17.25	1	0
Brock Red	7	55	7.86	1	0
Amblen White	10	97	9.70	2	0
	43	397	9.23	9	1

Ryan	Rushes	Yards	Yards/Carr	TD	PAT
West Randall	5	50	10.00	1	0
Anderson	10	30	3.00	0	0
Millersburg	7	51	7.29	0	0
Wonnace	4	16	4.00	0	0
Brock Red	10	72	7.20	1	0
Amblen White	9	25	2.78	0	0
	45	244	5.42	2	0

Isaiah	Rushes	Yards	Yards/Carr	TD	PAT
West Randall	5	24	4.80	0	0
Anderson	9	6	0.67	0	0
Millersburg	3	59	19.67	2	1
Wonnace	0	0	0.00	0	0
Brock Red	0	0	0.00	0	0
Amblen White	2	58	29.00	1	0
	19	147	7.74	3	1

Thomas	Rushes	Yards	Yards/Carr	TD	PAT
West Randall	2	18	9.00	1	1
Anderson	2	-3	-1.50	0	0
Millersburg	2	7	3.50	0	0
Wonnace	1	1	1.00	0	0
Brock Red	0	0	0.00	0	0
Amblen White	0	0	0.00	0	0
	7	23	3.29	1	1

Passing

Mateo	Comp	Att	Yards	TD	Int	PAT
West Randall	2	6	14	0	1	0
Anderson	6	10	54	1	0	0
Millersburg	4	8	58	1	0	1
Wonnace	8	15	85	1	0	0
Brock Red	4	10	19	0	0	0
Amblen White	7	10	23	0	1	1
	31	59	253	3	2	

Bloomville Pee Wee
2018 Tackles + Defensive Statistics

Name		West Randall	Anderson	Millersburg	Wonnace	Brock Red	Amblen White	Total	FF	FR	INT
Luke		4	0	3.5	1.5	6	2	17	1		
	TFL	4	0	2.5	0	3	1	10.5			
Gabe		3.5	2	2.5	2	3.5	3.5	17	2	2	
	TFL	2.5	2	1	0	0.5	0	6			
Wyatt		3	0	1.5	6.5	2	5.5	18.5		1	1
	TFL	1	0	0	0	0	0	1			
Jayden		2	0.5	1	3	1	2	9.5			
	TFL	2	0.5	0	0	1	1	4.5			
John		0	1	0.5	0	2.5	0	4		2	1
	TFL	0	0	0	0	0	0	0			
Anthony		1.5	1.5	2.5	5.5	1	1.5	13.5			1
	TFL	0	0	0.5	0.5	0	0	1			

Example of statistics recorded during a season

122   First-Time Coach: Youth Football

Keep it Cool

Nervous that you will not be able to conjure up a "win one for the Gipper" pregame speech to fire up the troops each week? Don't be. The truth is most coaches' addresses are not fit for the big screen. But that does not mean they are not important. During my time coaching I have taken part in addresses that are fiery, inspirational, strategic, optimistic, casual, serious, motivational, and funny. Each situation calling for you to address your team will be different. The main thing to remember as you approach these situations is to be yourself.

Pregame, be thorough but concise in reviewing tactics. Be sure to cover any position or assignment changes that may have come up because of absences or tardiness. Some motivational words will not hurt, but if your kids need a big speech from you to get excited, you have different issues. Chances are what you read as a lack of excitement is more likely some level of anxiety. Do your best to calm your kids' nerves by reminding them that they have done everything possible to prepare for this opportunity, and as such should be confident.

At halftime, be prepared to make tactical adjustments. You and your assistants will have seen things in the first two quarters that should be conveyed to your players. Be sure to also ask them what they are seeing. It often yields valuable intelligence. If things are going well, keep their heads in check and remind them they have two quarters to play against a team that is not going to quit fighting. If you are struggling, give them specific steps they will take to improve the situation. The situation will dictate whether you are a taskmaster, cheerleader, or somewhere in between.

Post-game, you will address the big picture of what happened, and give each of your assistants the chance to say a few words as well. An effective tactic is to ask your kids to offer their opinions of things they did well and things that did not. You will get some vague answers, and some that are flat-out wrong, but more often than not the kids know the reasons things turned out like they did. These positive reinforcements and critiques will be more meaningful coming from their peers.

PART 7

Postseason/ Offseason

Season's over. Now what? Hopefully your first year coaching was a good experience and you plan on doing it again. If you and your family were fully invested in football, chances are you spent the last two or three months grinding and could use a break. You should definitely take one! Go on a date night with your wife. Get cracking on the household projects that have been piling up since late summer. Read a book.

Before you completely check out and put football behind you for the year, make sure you wrap things up properly. Here are some late fall action items.

Banquet

Our organization holds a season-ending banquet each year, including our cheer and football teams. We start with our cheerleaders performing their competition routine, serve food and refreshments, and end with a program recognizing each kid, coaches, and others involved with the program. We give every child a poster featuring them in action during the season, as well as other prizes. This also serves as the primary equipment return date.

If your organization stages a similar event, this will be the last time you gather as a team. You probably will not have the time to speak at length about each individual player, but think of a way to make each kid feel special individually. One of our coaches enjoys giving a nickname to each player and introduces them like a pro wrestling public address announcer. Fun stuff! Recap the season's highs and lows for the assembled families, tell your players how proud you are of them, and thank the appropriate people.

Don't forget one big thing: Encourage your kids to keep playing football. That may seem obvious, or unnecessary, or not appropriate for such an occasion. Nonsense. Given the challenges tackle football faces from a variety of sources, you can not take for granted kids will continue playing. If you have provided a fun, safe, compelling experience for them throughout the season, it will not be a hard sell. But take this last opportunity you have with your players as a team to remind them (and their parents) of all the positives football offers.

If your organization does not hold a season ending banquet, look to hold a get-together for your team only, like a cookout at your house or swimming party at a local pool.

Review

At some point in the week following your last game, take an hour or two and jot down your thoughts on the season. Think about what went right and what went wrong. How can you build on and do more of the former, and correct the latter? How could you plan and run better practices? Were there consistent problems other teams gave you? Consider the kids you expect to be coaching next year and what positions they might play. Do they fit the offense and defense you ran this year, or will you need to tweak your schemes to fit your personnel? If you plan on making changes to your offensive or defensive playbook, draw up or articulate those changes as soon as possible.

For instance: in our most recently completed season, we ran a fair number of bubble screens but were not happy with the yardage they produced. Two weeks after our last game, we got a good view of how our high school team employs this concept out of a set similar to what we run. The next day I made the change in our playbook, and that is what we will implement next year.

Once you have aggregated your thoughts, share them with your coaches and ask for their feedback. Whether responding to your observations or contributing new ones of their own, more is better. While some of your thoughts may center around a specific theme, it is fine if they seem random and unconnected. This is a brainstorming session. As next season approaches you will need to decide which of these ideas are actionable and which can be left on the cutting room floor.

There are all sorts of ways to approach this exercise. Just do it. You may love football, but chances are you coach other sports like basketball, wrestling, or baseball. If you approach these with anything approaching your commitment to football, a significant chunk of your brain will be preoccupied with those sports during the football offseason. And that's great! Just like we encourage kids to play multiple sports and take part in other extracurriculars, coaching or supervising other sports or activities helps keep you well-rounded and helps prevent burnout. Just be sure to properly conclude your football season before moving on. If you don't, you might lose the benefit of some valuable experiences.

Continuing Education

The fact that you are reading a book on how to coach youth football suggests that you believe in educating yourself before undertaking important tasks. While it would be fantastic to claim this book contains so much youth football coaching information and wisdom that it is the only resource you will ever need on the topic, that is clearly ridiculous! We are firm believers in the value of lifelong learning, and coaching is no exception to this philosophy.

The best coaches never stop seeking out new information or better ways to do things. Fortunately, for such a competitive profession, the coaching fraternity is unusually generous in how it approaches information sharing. There is a long tradition of coaches opening their doors to coaching staffs, spending days explaining schemes and strategies.

Since you almost certainly have a full-time job outside of coaching, and since Nick Saban's thoughts on defense are probably a little much for your 9-year-old crew, paying visits to other coaching staffs is probably a little much. But there are plenty of night and weekend opportunities for you to broaden your coaching knowledge base and stay on the cutting edge of what is happening in the game.

Clinics and conferences: In Wisconsin, the Green Bay Packers and USA Football generously sponsor a free youth football coaches clinic each year. Held at Lambeau Field and the team's indoor practice facility, the event mixes big picture coaching philosophy with scheme-based sessions and on-field practice and technique periods. It is a perfect combination of ideas to bring back to our programs. Other well-known events include the USA Football national conference, clinics run by your state's football coaching association, and Glazier Clinics. Most of these are not free, and depending on your location may present travel challenges. But there is immense value in taking part in live, in-person education sessions and taking the opportunity to interact with clinicians.

Online: The aforementioned Glazier Clinics offers not only well-run live events, but also maintains a comprehensive collection of online clinics, webinars, and other football coaching educational opportunities. The cost for youth football coaches is quite reasonable, just $25 at time of this writing. USA Football offers a wide range of resources, including practice and training ideas, some free and some available via paid subscription. If you are interested in going deeper, X&O Labs is a membership-based website that delivers information on coaching trends, schemes, strategies, and drills.

YouTube was a great source of coaching ideas for me when I first started coaching and remains so today. My channel contains hundreds of youth football videos ranging from clinic reports to videos of our team's drills to game footage. There are countless other channels and videos with football coaching ideas, although not many are focused on youth football. If you are interested in chalk talk, Coach Mac, coach Ron McKie (different person), Joe Daniel Football, Coach Nate Albaugh, and others are great resources on a wide variety of topics. McKie, Daniel, and Keith Grabowski of USA Football all produce engaging podcasts, if you are looking for something to listen to in the car, while exercising, or mowing the lawn. If you are into Twitter, all of these guys are just some of the thousands of coaches who regularly share knowledge and opinions on social media.

Books: The one you are currently reading is just a tiny droplet in the collective ocean that is football coaching literature. Check out my Amazon page for an extensive collection of books about coaching football and other sports. Some in particular to get you going include *Developing an Offensive Game Plan* by Brian Billick, *Coaching the No-Huddle Offense* by G. Mark McElroy, *Coaching the RPO Offense* by Rich Hargitt, *The Hurry-Up, No-Huddle* by Gus Malzahn, and *Finding the Winning Edge* by Bill Walsh. These are all specific to the details of coaching football, but I also enjoy reading books about coaching innovators, like *The Perfect Pass* by S.C. Gwynne (about passing game guru Hal Mumme), or team building, like *The Captain Class* by Sam Walker. In a perfect world, reading for learning will become reading for enjoyment.

As you build your football coaching knowledge base, do not be afraid to contribute to the conversation. Pay it forward by helping other coaches broaden their knowledge base. Admittedly, it can be intimidating to jump into an X's and O's discussion with guys who have been coaching at high levels for years. Remember that even your limited experience and wisdom can seem vast to a coaching newcomer.

Never stop learning!

PART 8

Forward Pass

During spring of my older son's second grade year in school we signed him up to play tackle football that fall. We did not give it much thought. My son was a big boy who seemed to like sports, and football just seemed to be what kids in our small town did when they reached a certain age. My wife and I had little experience with the sport. Neither of her brothers played football. I played for two winless teams in middle school and high school while experiencing far greater success in baseball and basketball. In college I played for some really fun flag football teams and covered the University of Wisconsin football team as a reporter, but did not play tackle.

In what seems like the blink of an eye, many years have passed, and as I write this football has become arguably the centerpiece of our family's life. Our older son just concluded his freshman season as a member of our high school's first undefeated state championship team. It was an incredible fall that no one in our community will soon forget. Our younger son has one year left to play in our youth program, and has experienced a variety of key roles for his teams over the past three years. His first experience officially wearing the Firebird uniform was a scrimmage in front of 80,000 people at Lambeau Field!

My wife is our program's secretary, photographer, graphic designer, apparel coordinator ... you get the picture. She is our rock. In addition to serving as our local organization's president and a coach for my son's team, I am also president of our conference. These jobs encompass everything from equipment purchasing to scheduling, running meetings to marketing.

Both roles have been rewarding in their own way, and have afforded me the opportunity to meet a lot of great people. But nothing from the youth football experience has been as impactful as my time coaching.

On one hand there is the technical side of coaching: strategy, skill development, scouting, practice planning. Learning as much as possible about these things has become my hobby. Some guys hunt or work on cars. I watch Glazier Clinics videos and read X&O Labs.

On the other is the personal side of coaching: building relationships with kids and their families, with your fellow coaches, with your opponents. Some of my most vivid memories of my boys' childhoods have been celebrating their successes and consoling them after their setbacks. More than wins or losses, I will remember sixth graders getting teared up at their last practice or getting high fives from former players years later.

If you are lucky, football will provide you with a similarly rich experience.

Thank you for coaching, and good luck!

PART 9

Resources

Keep in Touch

Thank you for purchasing and reading this book! Below is a list of resources I have found useful in my time coaching youth football. First, here is my contact information — please feel free to contact me with questions or to share information about your coaching experiences. One of the best things about football is the spirit of community among coaches. Share what you know!

Email: scott_tappa@hotmail.com
Twitter: @scotttappa
Facebook: @scott.tappa.9, @isfirebirds
LinkedIn: @scotttappa

Documents and Files

A variety of useful document and file templates referenced throughout this book are available for download on the author's Google Drive, including a play sheet, play evaluation template, play count sheet, substitution plan, practice schedule, registration handouts, scout sheet, and wristband template.

https://drive.google.com/drive/folders/13xUiVmamM1BGXIEay3oi9v2zeJ3fwvan?usp=sharing

Books

Developing an Offensive Game Plan by Brian Billick
Coaching the No-Huddle Offense by G. Mark McElroy
Coaching the RPO Offense by Rich Hargitt
The Hurry-Up, No-Huddle: An Offensive Philosophy by Gus Malzahn
Football Scouting Methods by Steve Belichick
Finding the Winning Edge by Bill Walsh
The Perfect Pass by S.C. Gwynne
Playing Through the Whistle by S.L. Price
The Right Kind of Heroes by Kevin Horrigan
Must Win by Drew Jubera
Friday Night Lights by H.G. Bissinger
The QB by Bruce Feldman
The Essential Smart Football by Chris B. Brown
The Art of Smart Football by Chris B. Brown
The Captain Class by Sam Walker
114 Plays for Youth Football by Scott Tappa

Websites

USA Football, usafootball.com
Glazier Clinics, glazierclinics.com
X&O Labs, xandolabs.com
CoachTube, coachtube.com

YouTube Channels/Podcasts

Coach Mac
Ron McKie
Joe Daniel
Nate Albaugh
Keith Grabowski/USA Football

Twitter

@Youth_Football

@justplayfb

@txhsfbchat

@FBDevCoach

@CoachKGrabowski

@usafootball

PART 10

12 Simple Offensive Plays

Need to create an offensive playbook for your youth football team but at a loss where to start? Here are 12 simple plays to get you going: six runs, six passes. These plays do not constitute a system, but using these as a base you can create complementary concepts and plays that will be the basis for a diverse offensive attack. Remember that you do not need 100 plays at your disposal. The average youth football team will run 35-45 plays in a game with 8-minute quarters, so 25-30 total plays should suffice. Anything more than that and you will not have the time to rep them sufficiently.

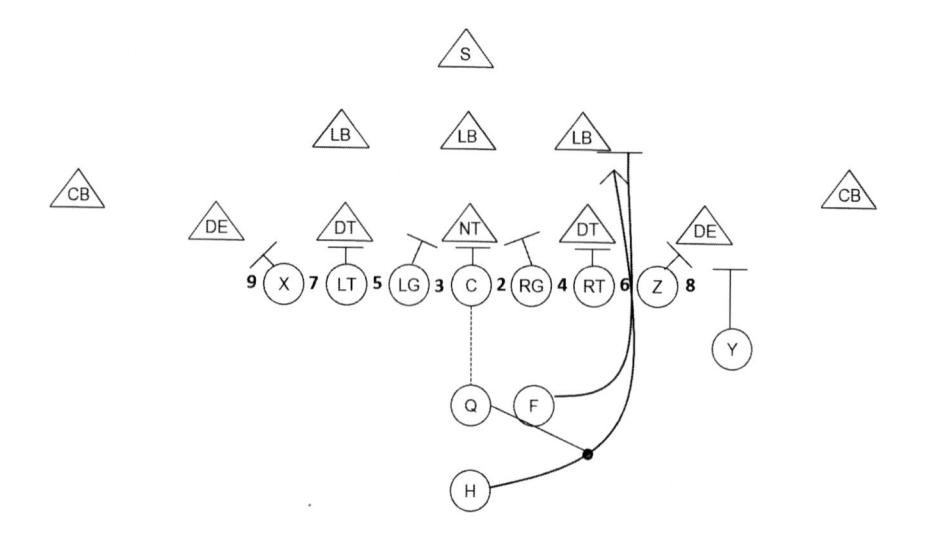

Gun Right 26 Lead

- Guards triple team NT with center, try to drive NT to second level; alternate: RG tags NT, climbs to MLB
- RT first step right foot, Z/TE first step left foot
- Y/TH double teams DE with Z/TE, boxing him in
- FB's first read is SLB
- HB makes cut off FB's block
- QB fakes bootleg after handoff

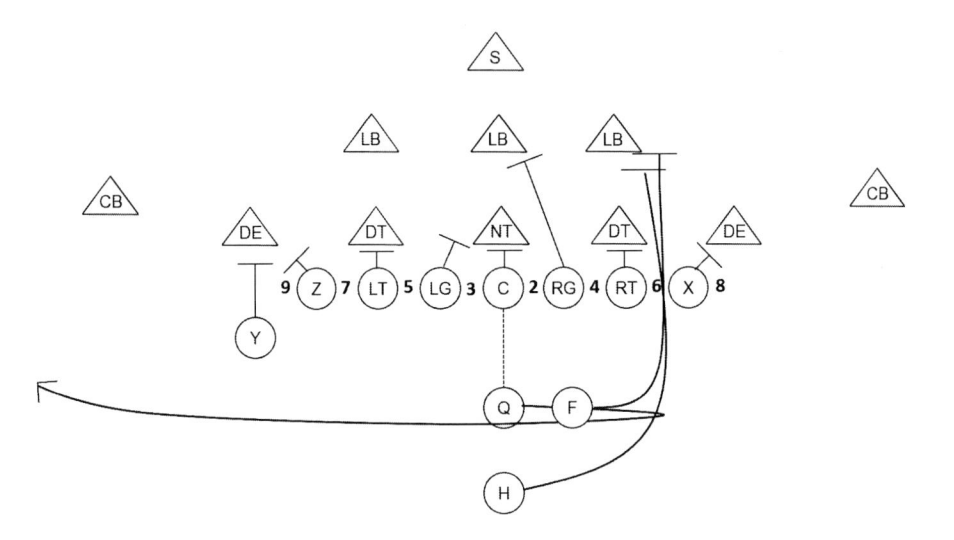

Gun Right 26 Bootleg

- Guards triple team NT with center, try to drive NT to second level; alternate: RG tags NT, climbs to MLB to sell 26 action
- LT first step left foot, Z/TE first step right foot
- Y/TH double teams DE with Z/TE, boxing him in
- QB fakes handoff to HB, makes tight turn after fake

Scott Tappa

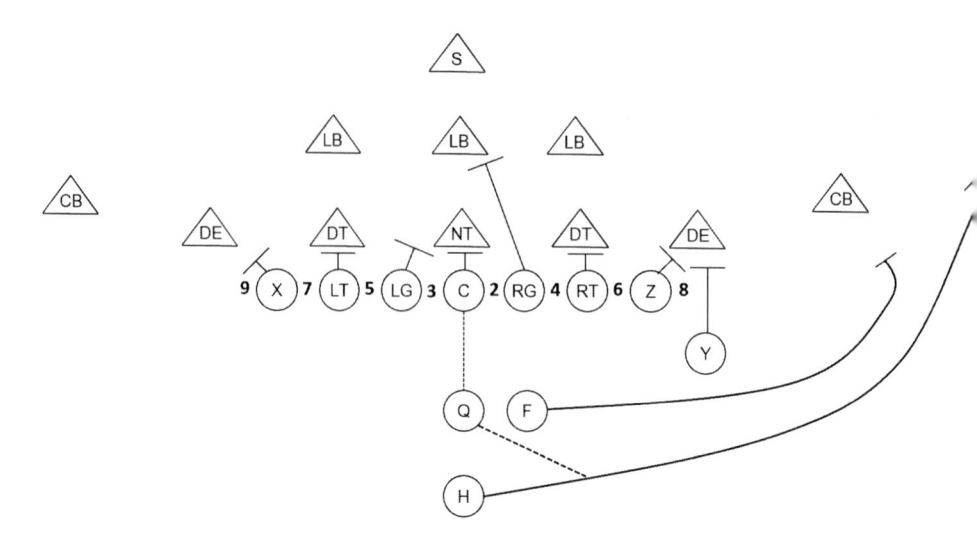

Gun Right 28 Sweep

- Z/TE's first priority is strong DE, double teaming with Y/TH
- If Z/TE has DE neutralized, Y/TH moves to SLB
- LG double teams NT, tries to push him to second level
- RG tags NT, moves to MLB
- FB picks up first dangerous defender, CB or SLB
- HB first steps are horizontal, gaining distance from QB
- QB makes eye contact with HB before making pitch, leading HB with toss
- QB fakes boot after pitch

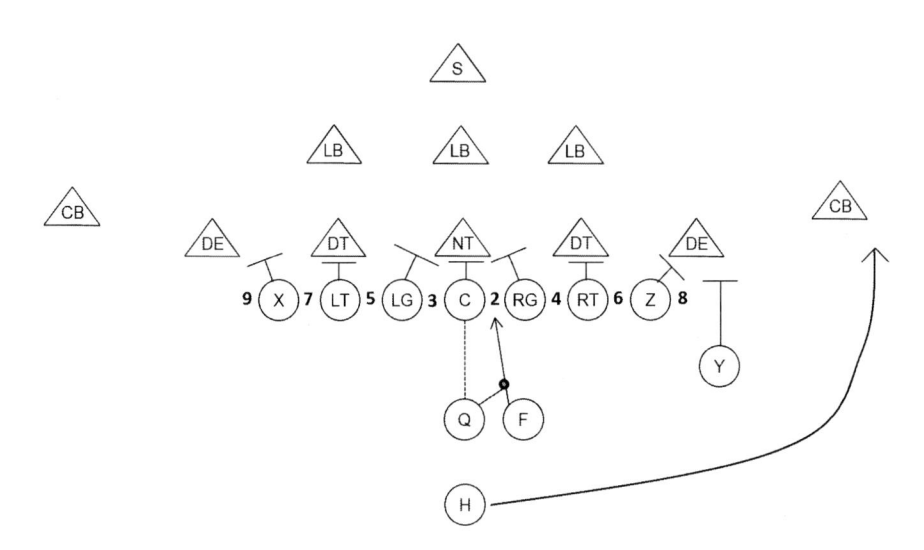

Gun/Strong Right 32 Dive

- Play best run with QB under center
- Guards and center triple team NT
- FB immediately gets arms in position to take handoff, hits hole as quickly as possible
- After handing to FB, QB fakes pitch to HB, who fakes catching pitch and executes 28 Sweep path
- RT first step with left foot
- Z/TE and Y/TH double team DE

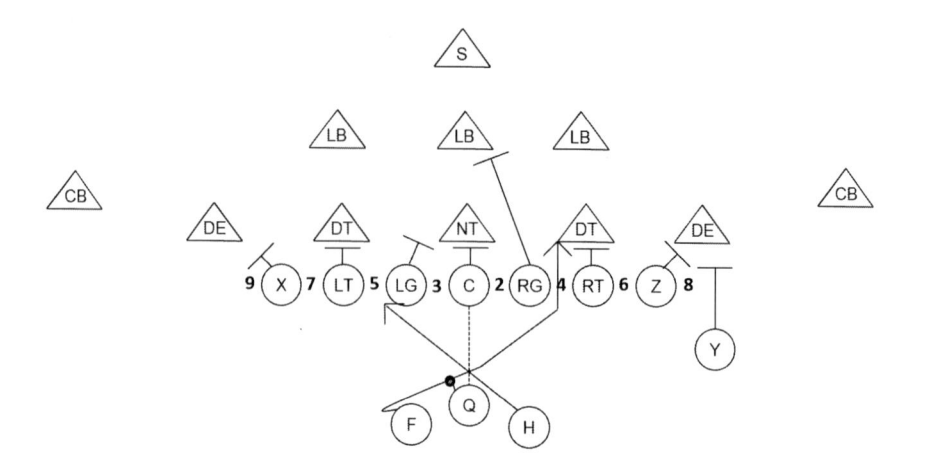

Pro Right 34 Crossbuck

- Best run with QB under center in Pro set — backs aligned behind guards
- HB and QB run fake 25 handoff
- FB takes jab step left simulating 25 lead blocking, then cuts back to receive handoff heading for 4 hole
- QB hands ball off with left hand
- LG double teams NT, tries to push to second level
- RG blocks MLB

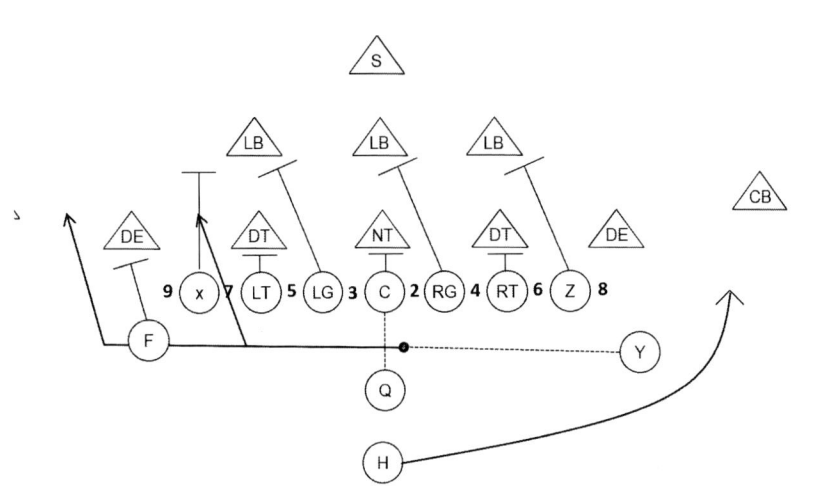

Jet Sweep

- Y/TH goes in motion on "set"
- QB times snap to hand ball off to Y in stride — inside handoff with left hand between him and line of scrimmage
- Aligned as tight wing, FB kicks out DE
- X/SE tags DE or DT before moving to block RLB
- Y/TH reads best available hole, 7 or 9
- HB fakes 28 pitch

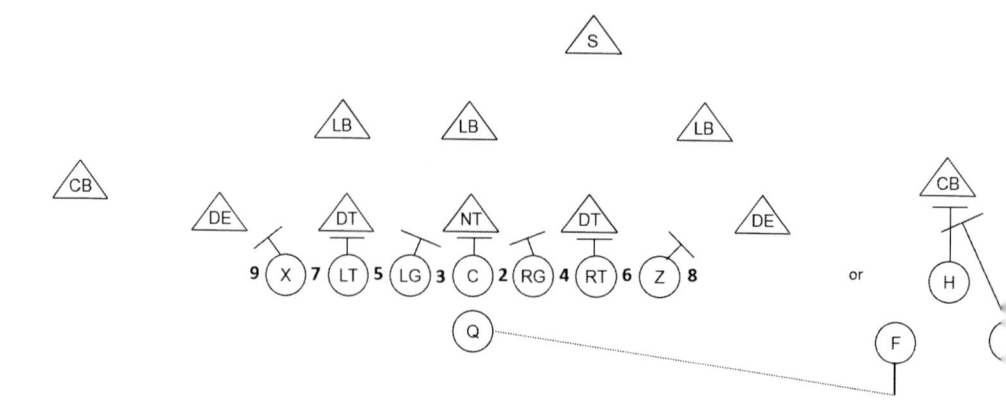

Trips Right Bubble Screen

- FB is primary, and only, receiver
- FB takes one step back on snap and raises hands
- QB's pass to FB is probably lateral — if not caught it is a live ball and must be recovered
- Blocking assignments contingent on how defense aligns to defend Trips formation
- HB blocks nearest defender, most likely CB, to inside
- Y/TH blocks second defender, S, DE, or SLB
- Z/TE blocks closest remaining defender — DE, SLB, or other
- Line pass blocks

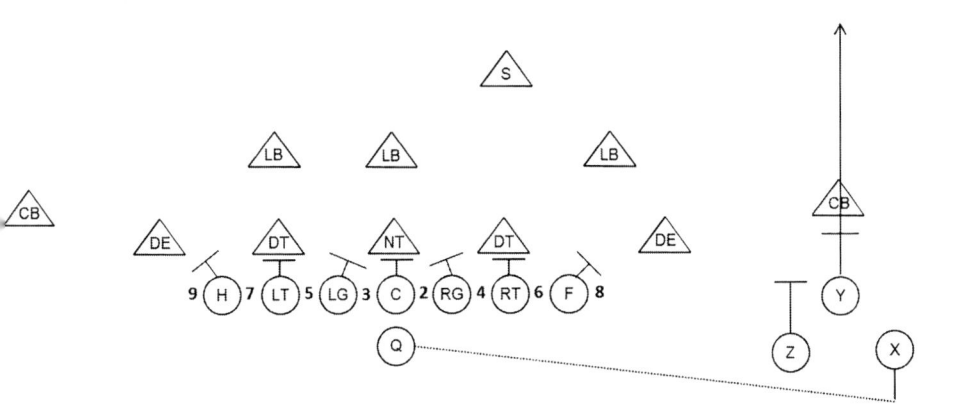

Trips Right Bubble and Go

- X/SE takes one step back behind Z/TE and Y/TH on snap, raises hands
- QB's pump fake pass to X/SE, who sells fake catch
- Y/TH chips CB to indicate bubble screen block, then releases on Go route
- Z/TE stays in place
- Line pass blocks

Scott Tappa 145

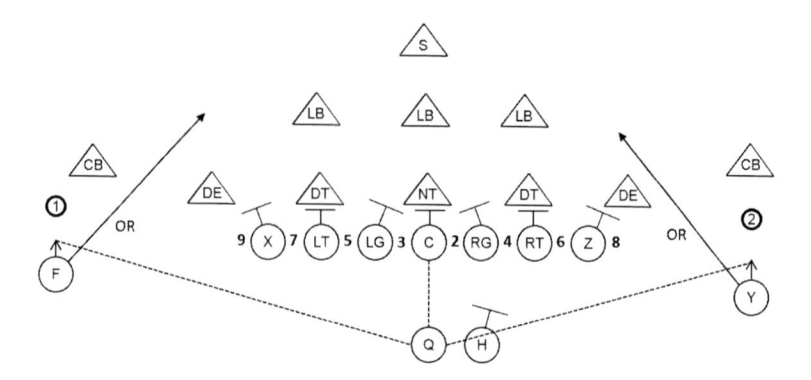

Slots Quick Hit

- FB (or HB) and Y/TH both split out — FB can shift or motion to spot if appropriate
- Receiver to wide side splits all the way out to numbers
- QB takes snap and immediately throws to wide side receiver, or receiver with more favorable CB matchup
- Run out of shotgun if possible
- Against pressing CB, can audible to quick slant or Go route (verbal call or tap helmet)
- HB pass protects, picking up first free pass rusher
- Line pass blocks

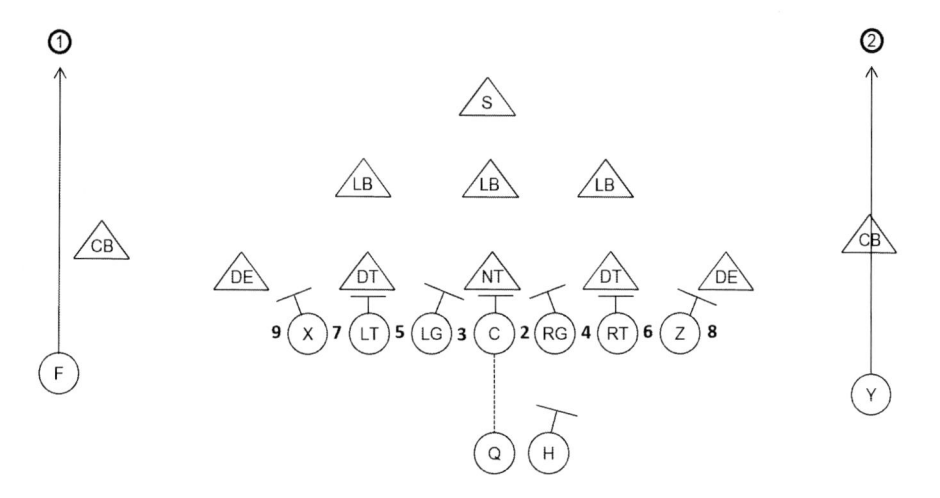

Slots Two Verticals

- FB (or HB) and Y/TH both split out — FB can shift or motion to spot if appropriate
- Receiver to wide side splits all the way out to numbers
- Split receivers both run Go routes at full speed, taking inside release
- QB takes snap and throws deep to receiver with more favorable CB matchup
- Throw should be to receiver's inside shoulder
- HB pass protects, picking up first free pass rusher
- Line pass blocks

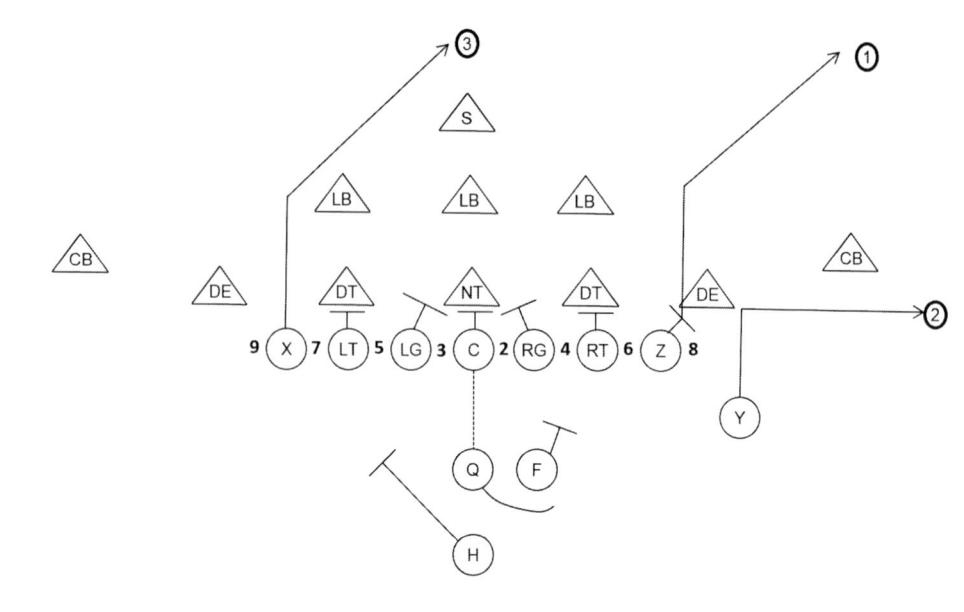

Tight End Pass

- Line pass blocks
- Z/TE runs 5-yard corner — 45-degree angle, cut with left foot
- X/SE runs 5-yard post or drag — or can stay in and pass block, depends on OL and opponent
- Y/TH runs flat
- HB and FB pick up first free pass rusher, HB to left, FB to right
- QB rolls out slightly to right to create clear passing window
- If possible run out of shotgun to allow QB better read of receivers/defense

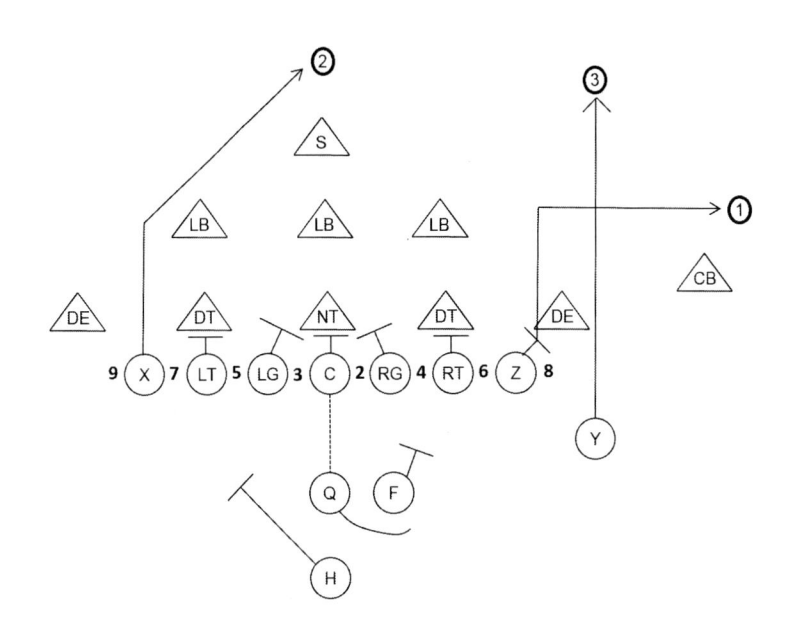

Tight End Pass Flip

- Line pass blocks
- Y/TH runs Go route, right at CB — full sprint
- Z/TE runs out into space vacated by CB, most likely 3 to 5 yards, then runs out — 90-degree angle, cut with left foot
- X/SE runs 5-yard post or drag — or can stay in and pass block, depends on OL and opponent
- HB and FB pick up first free pass rusher, HB to left, FB to right

ALSO FROM THIS AUTHOR

114 Youth Football Plays

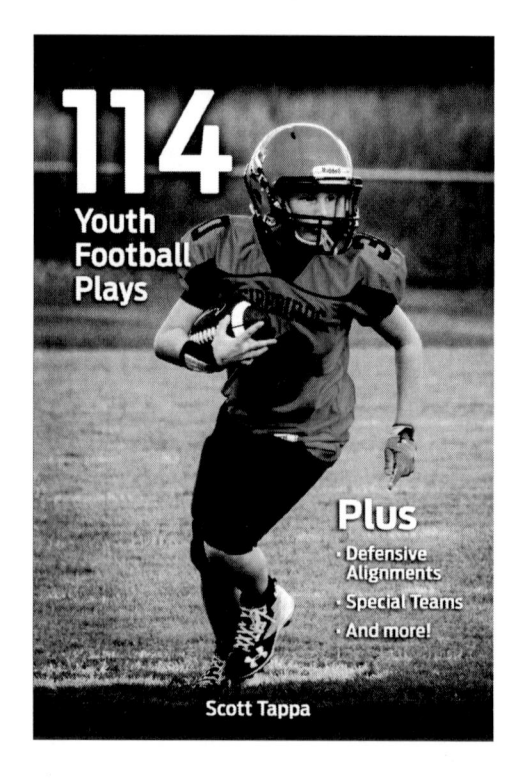

The world of offensive football is exciting, and vast.

Where does a coach looking to build a youth football playbook start? From veteran coach Scott Tappa, *114 Youth Football Plays* includes a wide variety of running and passing plays encompassing multiple concepts and formations. These complementary plays have proven to be effective for tackle football players age 8 through 12. In these pages you will find plays that will fit any coach's philosophy and any team's personnel. Each play is diagrammed, each player's assignment detailed. In addition, this book includes eight defensive formations, suggested special teams alignments, and more!

Made in United States
North Haven, CT
26 August 2025